Basic CANOEING

All the Skills and Tools You Need to Get Started

Jon Rounds, editor

Wayne Dickert,
paddling consultant

Photographs by
Skip Brown

Illustrations by
Taina Litwak

STACKPOLE
BOOKS

Copyright © 2003 by Stackpole Books

Published by
STACKPOLE BOOKS
5067 Ritter Road
Mechanicsburg, PA 17055
www.stackpolebooks.com

Printed in China

10 9 8 7 6 5 4 3 2

First edition

Photographs by Skip Brown
Illustrations by Taina Litwak
Additional photos by Alan Wycheck (paddles and gear,
    pp. 12, 66–69); Pat McConnell, NOC (pp. 39–40);
    Jon Rounds (dam, p. 46; p. 63)
Photos of Dagger canoes (pp. 2, 64) courtesy of Watermark
Cover design by Tracy Patterson

Library of Congress Cataloging-in-Publication Data

Basic canoeing : all the skills you need to get started / Jon
Rounds, editor ; Wayne Dickert, paddling consultant ;
photographs by Skip Brown; illustrations by Taina Litwak.
        p. cm.
Includes bibliographical references (p.   ) and index.
    ISBN 0-8117-2644-4
1. Canoes and canoeing. I. Rounds, Jon.
    GV783 .B375 2002
    797.1'22—dc21
                                                          2002012182

    ISBN 978-0-8117-2644-3

Contents

Acknowledgments

Since its founding in 1972, the Nantahala Outdoor Center in the Great Smoky Mountains of western North Carolina has been a magnet for the finest paddlers and teachers in the sport, and over the years the NOC has become synonymous with excellence in canoeing and kayaking instruction. Wayne Dickert, current head of instruction at Nantahala, is the latest in a distinguished line that includes Gordon Grant, Slim Ray, and Kent Ford. Like his predecessors, "Wayner," as he is known to fellow boaters, is both a world-class paddler and a world-class teacher. He is also a world-class person, and it was a pleasure working with him on this book.

It was likewise a pleasure working with photographer Skip Brown, who brought a rare combination of talents to the project. A competitive paddler himself, Skip understands the subject like few in the trade and is always ready to do whatever it takes to get the shot. Thanks also to:

Horace Holden, Wayne Dickert's Olympic paddling partner, for help demonstrating river moves.

Kent Ford, for review of the text.

Gordon Black, head of safety and instruction, American Canoe Association, for answers to questions on technique and safety.

Mary Liskow and Doug Gibson of Blue Mountain Outfitters, for the loan of equipment and the gift of advice. Located on the Susquehanna River in Marysville, Pennsylvania, just above Harrisburg, Blue Mountain has a huge inventory of canoes, from handmade wooden masterpieces to all-purpose Royalex boats, and is a must stop for paddlers anywhere in the area.

Mike Steck and Cheryl Cendrowski of Watermark, for providing images of Dagger canoes.

Finally, special thanks to Tracy Patterson, book designer, for her creativity and vision; and also to art director Caroline Stover and illustrator Taina Litwak.

—Jon Rounds

Introduction

The canoe's basic design has remained unchanged for centuries because the long, open, double-pointed hull continues to do certain things better than any other craft. It's lightweight and portable, it cuts through the water, it can carry a good deal of cargo, and it can be paddled by one or two paddlers facing forward. No other boat does all these things as well.

The canoe's enduring popularity is also a function of its simplicity. You pick the boat up and put it in the water: no trailer, no gas, no tune-up, no battery charge. And once afloat, a well-trimmed canoe in the hands of a good paddler is one of the sweetest things you'll see on the water.

Paddling a canoe, however, is deceptively simple. Although with no formal training, anyone can sit down and move the boat forward, learning good body mechanics and paddling principles in the beginning reaps immediate and lasting rewards. You'll be able to paddle farther with less muscle strain and you'll have much better control of the boat. You'll also be safer.

This book is for the beginner who wants to learn sound technique. It focuses on skills: thorough, graphic instruction on the paddling fundamentals and the essential strokes and maneuvers that apply to all types of canoeing. It also provides a guide to canoe types and gear and the basics of safety and rescue that every paddler must know.

Whether you aspire to river running, wilderness touring and camping, racing, or just paddling around a lake, the skills shown here will provide a solid foundation for a lifetime of paddling pleasure.

1

Fundamentals

Read this chapter before you pick up a paddle. It contains the basics that will get you on the water with the least amount of trouble and start you off paddling with good form. The first thing you'll have to do is carry the boat down to the water and launch it, and though this isn't rocket science, a number of things can go wrong that are easily prevented. You will then have to decide where in the boat to sit or kneel—simple deci- sions, but ones that make a big difference in how your canoe performs. And finally, take a few minutes to study the stroke mechanics outlined at the end of the chapter. These fundamentals of movement and posture are so basic and universal that understanding them from the start may be the single most valuable lesson in your paddling education.

Lifting and Carrying a Canoe

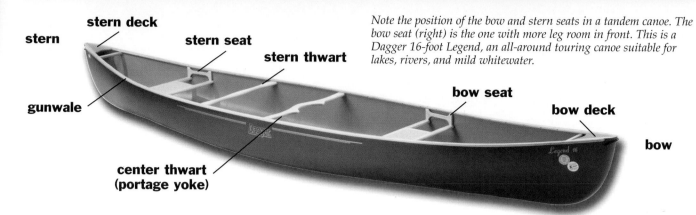

stern deck
stern
stern seat
stern thwart
gunwale
center thwart
(portage yoke)

bow seat
bow deck
bow

Note the position of the bow and stern seats in a tandem canoe. The bow seat (right) is the one with more leg room in front. This is a Dagger 16-foot Legend, an all-around touring canoe suitable for lakes, rivers, and mild whitewater.

One of the big advantages of a canoe is its portability. Even a small person can carry a canoe some distance and put it on the roof of a car. And a canoe can be carried between lakes or rivers on wilderness trips, giving you access to much more water than you'd have in a heavy boat that has to be hauled from the water at a boat ramp and driven around on a trailer.

At some point, then, you will be picking up a canoe and carrying it somewhere. Knowing the basics of lifting and carrying a boat will help you get on the water with the least amount of hassle.

TWO-PERSON CARRY

Two people can easily carry a canoe right-side-up by standing on opposite sides and grasping the bow and stern decks. This method is fine for carrying the canoe a short distance, from car to water, for example, but it's awkward walking on either side of a canoe for longer distances, and a narrow path may not have enough width to permit this method.

Two people, one on either side holding bow and stern deck, can carry a canoe a short distance comfortably.

SOLO OVERHEAD CARRY

Carrying a canoe solo on your shoulders is the preferred method for longer carries. Walking is less awkward with one set of legs under the canoe—you can more easily navigate around obstacles and the turns in a wooded path. And if the load is balanced and you have some padding on your shoulders, one person can comfortably carry even a large canoe a good distance. Touring canoes have a wooden portage yoke in the center

that's shaped to fit behind your neck. If you're carrying the canoe a long way, put a towel or other padding between your shoulders and the yoke.

For long portages on canoe camping trips, partners typically split the chores, one carrying the canoe and the other the gear. In cases where there's not much gear or where neither person can handle a canoe alone, two people can do an overhead carry by putting the canoe on their shoulders at bow and stern thwarts. This is somewhat more cumbersome than a solo carry, though, because you have to coordinate your steps. There's also less visibility because the bow person can't tilt the canoe back to see, as a solo carrier can. But it works. Two methods of getting the canoe on your shoulders are the *walk-under* (below) and the *amidships flip* (facing page). The walk-under requires less muscle. With the canoe upside-down on the ground, face the stern, lift the bow over your head, and step under it.

Holding the gunwales with either hand, walk hand-over-hand until you reach the middle of the canoe. Then turn around so you're facing front and tilt the boat onto your shoulders. If you have a partner, he can lift one end while you simply walk under the canoe at the center.

The easiest way to get a canoe onto your shoulders for a solo carry is to have someone lift the bow while you walk under the center. The partner then steadies the boat while you position your shoulders underneath the portage yoke and stand up.

AMIDSHIPS FLIP

The amidships flip is a quick, efficient way to get a canoe onto your shoulders. The heavier and larger the canoe, the more difficult this move can be, but if you get the setup and timing right, you don't need brute strength. The hardest part is the final move, where you lift the boat and roll it onto your shoulders. The setup to this can be done slowly, as separate steps, but once you get the canoe onto your thighs and are ready to flip it onto your shoulders, do it in one quick, smooth motion.

To get the canoe down off your shoulders, simply reverse the steps shown in the sequential photos. This procedure is easier, because you only have to lift the canoe a little ways to get it off your shoulders, roll it down onto your thighs (Step 5), and then set it gently on the ground.

1. With the canoe sitting flat on shore, grasp the near gunwale with both hands.

2. Pull the canoe up on its side, bottom toward you, and reach across and grasp the center thwart with both hands. (See next photo for position of hands.)

3. Bending at the knees, lean back and pull the canoe up onto your thighs.

4. Keeping the boat's weight on your thighs, continue turning it toward you until you can move your far hand from the thwart to the far gunwale. At this point, the weight is still on your thighs, but you're poised to flip the boat. Do the next two steps as one continuous motion. Keep your back straight throughout.

5. Stand up straight, bumping the canoe up off your thighs and taking the weight onto your lower hand . . .

6. . . . and flip the boat over onto your shoulders.

7. Settle it on your shoulders with the crook of the portage yoke right behind your neck.

Launching and Landing

There's nothing difficult about launching a canoe, but an unloaded craft is tippy, and a misstep can put you in the drink. The American Canoe Association recommends maintaining three points of contact on the canoe while boarding: two hands and one foot, or vice versa. Always place your steps along the centerline, not the edges, of the hull.

To save wear on the hull and to improve launching stability, the canoe should be fully afloat before being loaded or entered. Don't load a canoe on shore and shove it into the water or load it in water so shallow that the hull scrapes bottom. If the water's not deep enough right at the shore, walk the canoe out a little ways before getting in or loading.

A note on tandem boarding: Because the ends of a symmetrical canoe are identical externally, it may not be apparent to beginning paddlers which is the bow and which the stern. The clue is the positioning of the seats: the bow seat has more room in front of it for your legs (see photo, page 2).

BROADSIDE LAUNCH

This is a handy position for entering and loading because the full length of the canoe is alongside the shore or dock. To do a broadside launch without wading, however, the water must be deep enough right at the shoreline to float the boat.

With the stern paddler steadying the boat from shore or dock, the bow paddler steps in, placing the paddle across the gunwales as a brace, and gets down into his paddling position. The bow paddler then steadies the boat by holding the dock or shore while the stern paddler gets in.

For a solo launch, stand beside the boat at the point you will kneel or sit, and board using the same paddle-bracing technique. Get right down into your paddling position.

In a broadside launch, the stern paddler steadies the boat from dock or shore while the bow paddler gets in, placing the paddle across the gunwales as a brace.

BOW-FIRST LAUNCH

Along a wooded or rocky shore there may not be enough room to position the canoe for a broadside launch. Also, when waves are crashing parallel to shore, a broadside launch risks swamping the boat. In such cases, use a bow-first launch.

With the bow of the canoe pointing out from shore and the stern paddler steadying the boat from the rear, the bow paddler steps in and walks forward down the center, leaning over and holding onto the gunwales, until he reaches his seat. The stern paddler then gets in.

In a bow-first launch, the stern paddler steadies the boat while the bow paddler steps in and walks forward down the center to his seat, holding the gunwales.

LAUNCHING IN MOVING WATER

When boarding a canoe in a river, steady the boat by holding the upstream end. If you hold the downstream end, the boat will swing out into the current.

LANDING AND EXITING THE CANOE

In a broadside landing, one paddler gets out and steadies the canoe against the shore or dock while the other gets out.

In a bow-first landing, don't push the canoe too far onto shore. Walking on the bottom of a grounded canoe, or one in which the bow is resting on land, can damage the hull. Also, a canoe with any curvature to the bottom is very unstable on land. Nose the bow onto shore just enough to keep it from drifting away, leaving as much of the hull in the water as possible. Then walk forward in the same posture as in a bow-first launch, leaning over with hands on gunwales.

Trim and Pivot Point

Trim refers to how level a boat sits in the water, both fore and aft and side to side. A trim boat is completely level—neither bow nor stern sticks up higher than the other and the boat isn't tilted to either side. An easy way to check trim once paddlers and gear are in place is to pour a little water in the canoe and watch where it collects. In practice, canoes are seldom perfectly trim. A solo paddler, simply because of his position, tilts the boat toward his paddle side. Likewise, a canoe is often leaned into a turn. In fast water, many paddlers prefer a slightly bow-light canoe, for maneuverability. However, a boat that is significantly out of trim fore or aft is unwieldy and even dangerous. A bow-heavy boat tends to plow into the water, and a stern-heavy boat is difficult to steer.

Trim is directly related to a boat's *pivot point*, the point around which the boat turns. Several variables affect the pivot point: the position of the paddler or paddlers, the weight distribution of the gear, and the design of the hull.

A lone paddler in the stern of a tandem canoe—a common beginner mistake—is a classic example of how trim and pivot point affect boat handling. This paddling position creates a rearward pivot point and a severely out-of-trim boat that is impossible to control in wind or current. The paddler's weight sinks the stern and lifts the bow, and when wind (or current) catches the canoe broadside, it spins the hull with too much leverage for the paddler to counteract. The solution is simple: move the pivot point forward. For a solo paddler in a tandem boat, this means kneeling in front of the bow seat and facing the stern, creating a more central pivot point and a trim boat that is much easier to control. This also has the advantage of putting the paddler where the hull is wider and more stable.

Similarly, tandem paddlers may need to make adjustments to get their boat in trim. If the bow paddler is significantly lighter than the stern paddler, some gear can be moved forward to bring the bow down. If there is no gear to shift, the paddlers can move the bow seat back and/or the stern seat forward. If the seats are fixed, the paddlers will have to use the kneeling position and move slightly fore or aft.

This tandem canoe is trim, fore and aft. Neither bow nor stern sits higher than the other. Paddlers can adjust trim by moving slightly forward or back or by shifting gear fore or aft inside the canoe.

A paddler in a solo canoe kneels near the center of the canoe to keep it trim.

A solo paddler in the stern seat of a tandem canoe lifts the bow out of the water, putting the boat severely out of trim.

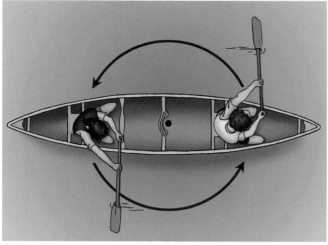

The pivot point is the axis around which the boat turns. Tandem paddlers should position themselves so this point is in the middle of the boat.

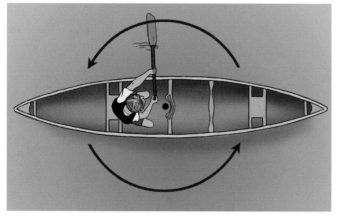

A solo paddler in a tandem canoe should sit in or kneel in front of the bow seat and face the rear. This puts the pivot point nearer the center of the canoe.

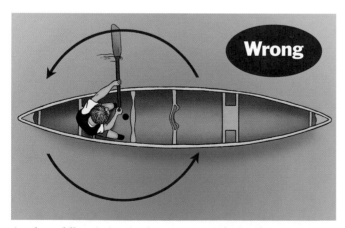

Wrong

A solo paddler sitting in the stern seat of a tandem canoe creates a pivot point too far to the rear. Because of the length of hull in front of him, he lacks the leverage to turn the boat into even a moderate wind, which will spin the boat like a weather vane.

Kneeling vs. Sitting

Experts are unanimous that for boat control, stroke efficiency, and safety, kneeling is better than sitting. Kneeling lowers your center of gravity, allows greater rotation of your torso, and puts more of your body in contact with the hull. Always use this position when paddling in rapids or in rough water on lakes. Spread your knees as far apart as comfortable and rest your butt against the seat or thwart behind you. Kneeling pads or a kneeling saddle make this position much more comfortable and also give you more control by keeping your knees from sliding around on the bottom of the canoe.

But there are times when sitting is just fine. Most people find it more comfortable than kneeling, and if you're just out for a relaxing trip across calm water, sit and paddle to your heart's content. You can also sit periodically as a break from kneeling on a long haul across open water.

Kneeling position. *Kneel with your legs as far apart as comfortable and your butt resting against the seat or thwart behind you.*

Paddling Body Mechanics

The key to powerful, efficient, injury-free paddling is to perform strokes using the large muscles of your torso rather than the smaller muscles of your arms. The following points will help you develop a sound paddling technique. Although discussed separately here, these fundamentals are closely related and become inseparable once you've developed a fluid stroke motion.

• Sit up straight and flex at the waist

You can lean slightly forward for a power stroke, but keep your back straight and avoid leaning too far and reaching with the arms. The straight-up posture keeps you centered over the boat and in better balance, resulting in a smoother, more powerful stroke and a more stable canoe.

• Rotate your torso during strokes, rather than reaching with your arms

To illustrate this concept, stand up straight in a room and extend your arm so your fist is six inches from the wall. Keeping your arm straight, touch the wall by rotating at the waist. Imagine this translated to a paddling motion. Your arms just connect your torso to the paddle; it's the torso that delivers the power.

Good form. *The paddler's back is straight and the right side of his torso is rotated forward to plant the paddle for a forward stroke. Note that the paddle blade is farther forward than in the photo below. This stroke will derive its power from the paddler unwinding his torso.*

Bad form. *The paddler is hunching forward and reaching with his arms. Despite this effort, the paddle blade is not as far forward as in the photo above. This stroke will rely for its power on the paddle being pulled through the water. It will be much less effective than one driven by torso rotation.*

• Keep your weight centered over the boat

This is the key principle to achieving balance in a canoe. Your center of gravity is somewhere around your navel. Keep your head over this point and this point, in turn, over the center of the boat. When you need to lean the boat, do so with your lower body—by sinking or raising a knee—rather than by extending your torso over the gunwale. Lean the boat, not your body.

• Keep your hands and arms within the paddler's box

The height of this imaginary box is from the gunwale to the top of your head. It is as wide as the span between your hands in a normal paddle grip and extends from your back to as far in front as you can reach with your back straight. The box rotates as your torso rotates. Visualizing the box and keeping your hands within it will help prevent shoulder injuries. It will also remind you to rotate your torso when placing the paddle behind you, rather than reaching back with your arms.

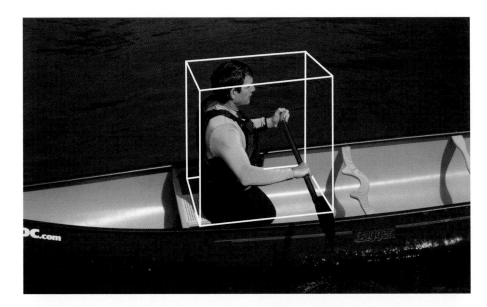

Paddler's box. *This imaginary box is shoulder-width and extends in front of the paddler's torso as far as he can reach and from the gunwale to his head.*

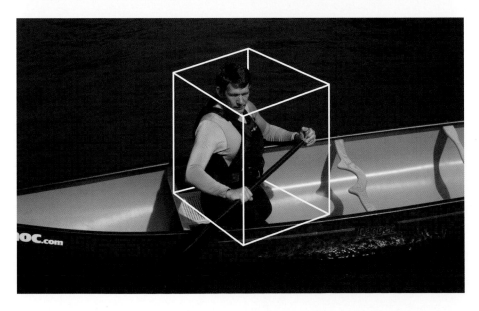

The box rotates with the paddler. Keep your arms within the box and get them where you need them by rotating your torso, rather than by reaching outside the box.

Notice how the paddler follows the blade of the paddle with his head, leading his torso around to the rear.

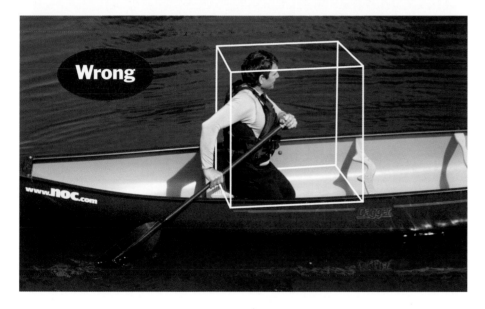

Reaching outside the box is one of the main causes of shoulder injury. It's also inefficient stroke technique.

• Plant the paddle and move the boat

Rather than thinking of the water as a liquid through which you pull the paddle, think of it as a stiff substance into which you completely submerge the blade in order to draw the boat forward. You are moving the boat, not the paddle. Visualizing a power stroke in this way—as pulling the boat forward using the paddle as an anchor and torso rotation for torque—discourages arm paddling. It also illustrates why a forward stroke is begun as far forward as possible and ends alongside your hips rather than behind you. The farther forward you plant the blade, the farther you can pull the boat with your unwinding torso. Conversely, continuing a forward stroke behind your body is inefficient: you're just lifting water with the paddle.

5 Telltale Signs of Incorrect Posture and Paddling Movement

1. Bent arms (indicates arm paddling)
2. Excessive hip shifting (pulls boat off course)
3. Hunched-over upper body (shifts weight off center, puts boat out of trim)
4. Hands inside the boat (prevents vertical paddle placement and keeps paddle from traveling parallel to centerline)
5. Inactive shoulders (indicates lack of torso rotation)

Adapted from *The American Canoe Association's Canoe and Kayaking Instruction Manual* by Laurie Gullion. Used with permission of Menasha Ridge Press.

Vision

Another fundamental concept of paddling—one that cannot be photographed or diagramed but is common among all good canoeists—is looking ahead. Rather than focusing on the bow of the canoe or your grip on the shaft, look up toward where you want to go. If you're paddling across a lake, look to your destination on the far shoreline. You might focus on a tree to keep you on course and let you gauge the frequency of your corrective strokes. If you're running a river, look beyond the rock directly ahead and survey the entire rapid to where you'll emerge. See the big picture.

At the same time, be sure to look directly in front of your canoe now and then to check for unforeseen obstacles that may pop up. Particularly in more complex situations such as running a rapid, your best chance for success is constantly shifting your focus between the big picture and the details.

The habit of looking ahead extends naturally to the psychological technique of visualization, which many athletes use for better performance. A whitewater paddler will visualize himself navigating a complex rapid successfully and emerging below. Visualization prompts you to consider what's ahead and plants the idea of a successful outcome.

2

Forward and Corrective Strokes

Flatwater—the paddling term for a lake or a wide stretch of river with no current—is the ideal place to practice strokes. Whether or not you plan to ever paddle on moving water, begin here. Flatwater is best for learning strokes because it allows you to concentrate on what your paddle and body movement, not the current, are doing to the boat. It is also safer to stay off rivers until you've mastered basic strokes.

Instructors are divided about whether it is better to learn strokes solo or with a partner. On the one hand, canoes are traditionally tandem craft, and most people find paddling with a partner more fun. Also, a well-coordinated pair of paddlers can maneuver a canoe with great efficiency and power.

On the other hand, the mechanics of solo and tandem strokes are, in most cases, identical. A stroke is a stroke. The advantage of learning solo is that you can experience more directly a particular stroke's effect on the boat, whereas with two paddlers, you're feeling the combined effect of bow and stern strokes.

Basic strokes in this book are demonstrated by a solo paddler. With a few exceptions, the same techniques apply to tandem strokes.

Terminology

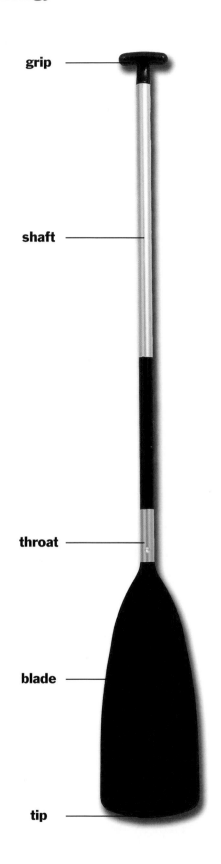

grip

shaft

throat

blade

tip

Parts of a Standard Paddle

Grip Hand and Shaft Hand. Grip the paddle with your top hand (grip hand) and lower hand (shaft hand) about shoulder-width apart. You'll raise and lower the shaft hand for different strokes. For a forward stroke, for example, your shaft hand will be down close to the blade, whereas for a sweep, it will be farther up.

grip hand

shaft hand

Control Thumb. The thumb on the grip hand is referred to in paddling instruction as the "control thumb" or "indicator thumb." It really doesn't control anything; it's just a signaling device that indicates which way the paddle is rotated. When learning strokes, keep your control thumb extended and follow the directions about which way it should point—up, down, forward, or back—when the paddle shaft is rotated in the right direction.

Extending the thumb on your grip hand is a handy device for indicating which way the paddle is rotated. Here, the control thumb is pointing up at the end of a stern pry. Had the paddler done a J-stroke, his thumb would be pointing down.

Powerface and Backface. The side of the blade that you pull toward yourself in a forward stroke is called the powerface, and the other side, the backface (or non-power face). Different strokes use different sides of the paddle for propulsion, and some use both. It will be easier to follow stroke instructions if one side of your paddle is marked as the powerface. Some paddles already have a logo or label on one side. If not, mark one side with a waterproof marker.

On-side and Off-side. The side of the canoe on which you place the paddle for a forward stroke (and all other strokes but cross strokes) is called your on-side, and the other side, your off-side. These terms are unique to canoeing because canoes are the only craft you paddle from one side. The terms are used in stroke instructions to indicate where to place the paddle and which way the boat turns, and also which direction to lean the boat in maneuvers. For example, you'll be told that a stern pry turns the boat sharply toward your on-side, or that you should lean into an eddy turn by weighting your on-side knee. Balance and weight distribution are such crucial issues in canoeing instruction, in fact, that on-side and off-side will become very familiar terms.

FORWARD STROKE

The forward stroke is the engine that drives the boat, and though instructors may be reluctant to admit it, even a lousy one does the job. Without any coaching on form, most people can paddle a canoe forward. An untrained forward stroke may not be graceful or efficient, and the boat may zigzag, but it will get you where you're going. However, if you paddle often or for any distance, you'll go farther and straighter with less effort if you learn good form at the start. And the forward stroke is an excellent place to start practicing the basic principles of posture and rotation that extend to all strokes.

Rhythm

Developing a fluid, powerful forward stroke is a matter of putting the various elements together with the right timing. At first, it all seems too much to keep in mind—body posture, torso rotation, paddle angle and distance of travel, exit and recovery. But sit back and watch a good paddler over some distance and you'll see all these elements come together in a compact, rhythmic motion that moves the boat in a straight line with what seems like very little effort. Because his stroke is short and powerful and he's not reaching with his arms, the paddler is probably making more strokes per minute than you realize. He plants the paddle vertically, brings it back forcefully in a short stroke parallel to the hull, and holds the corrective position (J-stroke or stern pry) for just the right beat before beginning the next stroke. And it all happens in a seamless, repetitive motion, like a well-oiled piston. If you really want to appreciate the value of good technique, try keeping up with him.

One Thing at a Time

Don't be discouraged if you can't put all the elements together right away. The most fundamental challenge of canoeing is achieving directional control while developing solid stroke technique: in other words, keeping the boat on course while getting power and efficiency from your strokes. It takes practice.

Concentrate first on getting the boat to go where you want it to. After you can do that, focus on individual parts of the stroke. Paddle a certain distance with the goal of rotating your torso and keeping your arms straight when you plant. Then concentrate on planting your blade vertically and moving it parallel to the hull, then on stroke length and slicing the blade from the water at the end of a stroke. Finally, experiment with the timing of your corrective stroke. As each of these elements are committed to muscle memory, you'll be able to put them together and move on to developing a stroke cycle with a rhythm of your own.

Forward and Corrective Strokes

Windup. Keeping your shaft arm straight and your grip hand at head level, extend the paddle as far forward as possible by rotating your torso. Keep your back straight and don't lean forward excessively.

Catch. Plant the paddle vertically in the water and push down with your grip hand. Don't start pulling back until the paddle blade is submerged to the throat. Your on-side shoulder should be rotated forward at this point. Your off-side shoulder remains stationary through the stroke, serving as the pivot point of torso rotation.

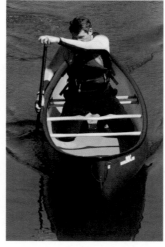

Propulsion. Rotate your torso forcefully with a burst of energy in the first six inches of the stroke. Imagine you are pulling the boat past a paddle planted in wet cement. Keep both hands away from the body and keep the paddle parallel to the centerline of the boat as you pull. If the blade is slanted and only half submerged, you won't get near the power you will from a vertical, fully submerged blade.

Exit. When the paddle is alongside your hips, slice it away from the hull . . .

. . . and remove it from the water by lifting your shaft hand and pulling your grip hand down. Exiting this way—with the edge rather than the flat of the blade pushing against the water—reduces water resistance.

CORRECTIVE STROKES

Canoes want to turn. A rowboat goes straight because the oars are mounted amidships and operate in mirror image on either side of the boat. But a canoe, being a long narrow shell propelled from the side, does nothing so easily as turn. Even with two paddlers doing identical forward strokes on opposite sides of the canoe, the boat will gradually turn away from the stern paddler's side because of the greater leverage from that end. And this turning effect is even more pronounced in a solo canoe. Some correction, then, is needed to maintain a straight course.

One solution is to switch sides every few strokes (see page 20). A smoother and easier way to keep the boat on course is for the stern paddler or solo paddler to use a corrective motion at the end of his forward stroke.

When you've learned both the strokes below, use the stern pry after the first few forward strokes from a standing start. Once the canoe is moving and headed where you want, switch to the J-stroke.

STERN PRY   Moves the bow back toward the on-side after a forward stroke

The stern pry is easy to learn and especially effective as a corrective stroke for swinging the bow back toward your on-side after the first few forward strokes from a standing start. It's a powerful stroke that you will also use by itself to turn the boat. Its one drawback as a corrective stroke is that it slows the forward momentum of the boat somewhat.

Finish your forward stroke past your hips (a bit farther back than you would for a normal forward stroke).

Rotate the shaft so the powerface of the paddle is facing the hull (control thumb pointing up and back) and hold the shaft of the paddle against the gunwale with your shaft hand. The paddle is now poised to pry the stern toward the paddler's off-side, thus pivoting the bow the other way, toward the paddler's on-side.

Rudder: If your boat is traveling forward fast enough, simply holding the paddle in this position—called a rudder—for a second will keep the boat from turning to your off-side. If you are moving slower or standing still, or if you need a sharper turn, continue with the pry.

Keeping the shaft pinned against the gunwale with your shaft hand, pull your grip hand across your chest (control thumb up) levering the blade, backface out, away from the hull. Don't let your shaft hand slide back along the gunwale during this phase, or you will, in effect, be doing a backstroke.

Stern Pry

backface

powerface

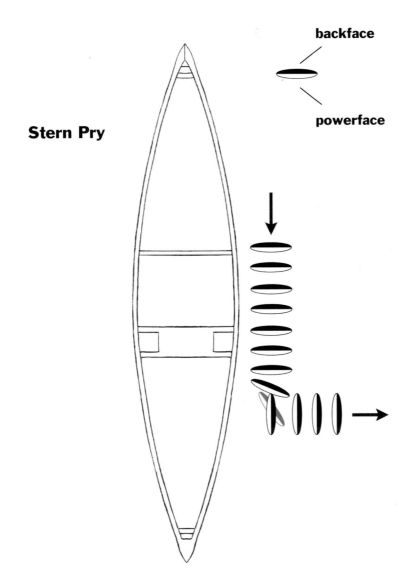

For the stern pry, rotate the paddle so the powerface points toward the hull and the backface pushes against the water during the stroke.

The J-stroke is so-named because the path of the paddle, viewed from overhead, traces the letter J. It is used for the same kind of correction as the stern pry—to turn the boat back toward the paddler's on-side at the end of a forward stroke—but it doesn't turn the boat as abruptly as the pry nor reduce its forward momentum as much. The J-stroke is thus most effective when the canoe is already underway, whereas the stern pry is better when starting a boat from a standstill.

The J-stroke takes practice to master because it involves rotating the wrist in an unnatural direction. But once mastered, it's a smooth stroke that fits seamlessly into a series of forward strokes and keeps the boat straight without slowing it down.

Forward and Corrective Strokes

At the end of the forward stroke . . .

. . . rotate your grip hand counterclockwise (control thumb down), causing the powerface of the paddle to turn away from the hull (the opposite of the stern pry), and . . .

. . . push the powerface of the paddle away from the hull with your shaft hand. Note how the control thumb is pointed down between the paddler's knees, the opposite of the stern pry.

backface

powerface

J-Stroke

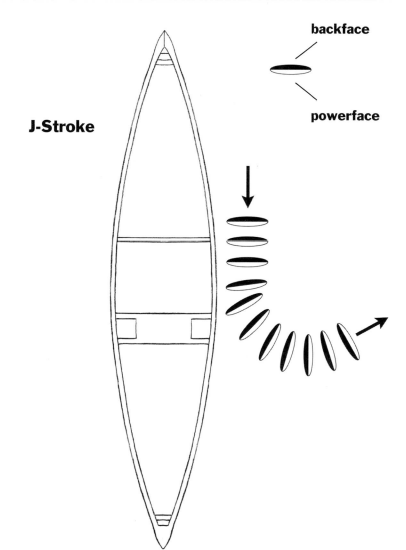

For the J-Stroke, rotate the paddle so the backface points toward the hull and the powerface pushes against the water during the stroke.

SIT 'N' SWITCH

As an alternative to corrective strokes, tandem paddlers or a solo paddler can keep a boat going straight by switching sides after a certain number of strokes. This method requires more energy than using corrective strokes, and good sit 'n' switch technique should not be confused with the frantic switching novice paddlers do to get a boat back on course. But a solid side-switching method does make the boat go a little faster over the long haul because the stern paddler is using pure forward strokes, with nothing wasted on corrective motions at the end of the strokes. In fact, the fastest marathon racing teams use this technique.

To get full efficiency when switching sides, completely finish the forward stroke on one side before lifting the paddle out of the water. Once it's out, flip the paddle far enough forward so it's in position for a new forward stroke on the other side of the boat. Don't do half a forward stroke on one side of the boat, and then pass the paddle over the boat close to your chest.

To coordinate the switching in a tandem canoe, the stern calls "switch" as the bow paddler begins a stroke, and then both cross over at the end of that stroke. Switching sides every ten to twelve strokes should keep the boat on course. A solo paddler will have to switch more frequently.

SIT 'N' SWITCH   A technique to keep a boat going straight without corrective strokes

Finish a normal forward stroke.

Lift the paddle out of the water . . .

. . . and flip it across the boat with your shaft hand (the bow paddler's left hand in this picture), releasing your top hand and . . .

. . . grasping the paddle underneath your shaft hand while moving your shaft hand up . . .

. . . to its new position as the top hand.

And begin a forward stroke on the other side.

ROLES OF BOW AND STERN PADDLER

Bow and stern paddlers have slightly different roles, and though you may gravitate to one end or the other, depending on your skills and inclinations, learn both positions. This will make you a better paddling partner, because you'll understand the difference between bow and stern strokes and how to complement your partner's moves. It will also make you more flexible for those times you're paired with someone who prefers the end you're used to. So it's a good idea to switch positions every few hours when you're learning.

Bow Paddler

The bow paddler is the navigator. He or she is generally responsible for power strokes and immediate turning decisions. Turning strokes themselves have more effect on the boat from the stern, but the bow paddler has a better vantage point from which to see the route ahead and spot hazards, so it is he or she who decides where the boat should go and communicates this to the stern. With experienced pairs, this communication becomes nonverbal; the bow paddler does a certain stroke and the stern automatically responds with a complementary stroke.

Stern Paddler

Steering strokes have more effect from the stern because the stern paddler has more hull in front of him and therefore more leverage. While the bow paddler does power strokes, it is the stern paddler who performs corrective strokes to adjust the boat's course over the long term. However, the stern paddler must be attentive to the bow paddler's moves or verbal directions—especially in rapids or passages with underwater hazards—and respond with complementary strokes.

3

More Strokes

Now you know how to move the boat straight ahead. With the strokes in this chapter, you'll be able to turn the canoe left or right, move it sideways or backwards, or spin it on a dime.

As you practice these strokes, apply the principles of body rotation, balance, and posture from Chapter 1. Keep your body upright and centered over the boat, follow the paddle shaft with your eyes, and generate power by rotating your torso rather than by reaching with your arms.

PRY STROKES

The stern pry is shown in Chapter 2 as a corrective stroke performed at the end of the forward stroke, but it is also used alone to pivot the bow sharply toward your on-side. It does this by pushing the stern the other way, toward your off-side. It's a short, quick, powerful stroke used by stern and solo paddlers, especially in river maneuvers such as eddy turns and on-side ferries (see pages 50 and 56).

In a tandem canoe, the pry is almost always a stern stroke. But a bow paddler can use it as a complement to a stern stroke in turning the canoe abruptly.

STERN PRY   Turns the bow sharply toward your on-side

Rotate your body toward your on-side and plant your paddle behind you, resting the bottom of your shaft hand on the gunwale. Your control thumb should be up and the backface of the paddle facing away from the hull.

Keeping your shaft hand right where it is (don't let it slide backward or forward on the gunwale), pull your grip hand across the boat in front of your chest, prying the backface of the blade away from the boat.

Continue prying, keeping your shaft hand where it is, until the blade is out of the water.

More Strokes

DRAW STROKES

A draw stroke pulls the boat toward the paddle—the opposite of a pry. It can be used to pull the boat sideways, or, if the paddle is drawn toward bow or stern, to pull one end of the boat around. Used in combination by bow and stern paddler, draw strokes can spin a boat in a tight circle. They are most commonly used alone, however, to make course corrections and quick turns in moving water.

STANDARD DRAW — Draws the boat sideways, toward the paddle

Rotate your torso toward your on-side and extend both arms over the water, perpendicular to the gunwale, and plant your paddle in the water with the blade as vertical as possible. Your control thumb should be pointing back toward the stern, the powerface of the paddle facing the boat.

Push down with your grip hand . . .

. . . and draw the boat toward the paddle by unwinding your torso. Think of it as pushing water under the boat.

Standard Draw (continued)

Before the paddle gets all the way back to the hull, rotate your grip hand outward, turning the paddle blade perpendicular to the hull . . .

. . . and slice it away from the boat to remove it from the water with less resistance. Here, the paddler is extending for another draw stroke.

With your grip hand so the control thumb is down, plant the paddle as you would for a standard draw, but angle the powerface of the blade toward the bow.

Move the paddle toward the bow . . .

. . . by rotating your torso.

Complete the stroke by bringing the paddle almost to the gunwale.

More Strokes

Rotate toward your on-side, as for a standard draw, and plant the paddle as far out as you can. Your shaft hand should be completely straight and your grip hand directly above the gunwale.

Draw the paddle back toward the stern, rotating your torso . . .

. . . and following the shaft with your eyes all the way. Watching the shaft will help you rotate.

Bring the paddle back as far as you can, until the shaft nearly touches the gunwale.

More Strokes

SWEEP STROKES

Sweep strokes are made in wide arcs, with the paddle reaching far from the pivot point of the boat. They are used to turn the boat while maintaining its forward momentum. Draws and prys also turn a boat, but the sideways effect of these strokes slows the boat's forward progress. A sweep, by contrast, turns a boat while still pushing it forward. This is a valuable feature in moving water, where forward momentum is key. Just as in riding a bicycle, you have more control of a turn when you keep the vehicle moving in the direction you want it to go, rather than stalling it. A stern paddler can use a forward sweep to help push a boat up into an eddy as the final move in an eddy turn. On a lake, a sweep will get the boat back on course when you need a bigger adjustment than a corrective stroke can make, or you can use a sweep for any major change of direction.

Sweeps are among the few strokes performed differently by solo and tandem paddlers. Although the form is the same, the solo version travels through a longer arc (almost 180 degrees) than the tandem counterpart (90 degrees).

SOLO FORWARD SWEEP — Turns the boat sharply to the off-side while maintaining its forward momentum

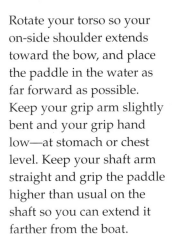

Rotate your torso so your on-side shoulder extends toward the bow, and place the paddle in the water as far forward as possible. Keep your grip arm slightly bent and your grip hand low—at stomach or chest level. Keep your shaft arm straight and grip the paddle higher than usual on the shaft so you can extend it farther from the boat.

Now unwind your torso...

... pushing out with your hands so both are over the water, and bring the paddle in a wide arc toward the stern. Following the paddle with your eyes helps you rotate your torso with the stroke.

Solo Forward Sweep (continued)

Note how far out from the boat the blade travels as it sweeps through its arc. The greater the distance from the pivot point, the greater the turning power of the stroke. From this point on, the stroke is the same as a stern draw.

Continue rotating until the paddle is well behind you, letting your shaft arm bend at the elbow as it moves behind your body.

Exit: Note how the paddler's head and torso are rotated toward the rear and his shaft arm is bent.

More Strokes

Rotate your torso toward the stern, shifting your weight to your on-side knee, and place the paddle in the water behind you. Keep both hands low, control thumb pointing up. Your shaft hand should be high on the paddle so you can place the blade farther from the boat.

Sweep the paddle forward in a wide arc, pushing against the water with the backface of the blade, with most of your weight still on your on-side knee. Follow the paddle with your eyes, so your head and torso rotate with the stroke.

When the paddle is across from your hips, it should be at its farthest point from the boat. Your weight now begins to shift back to your off-side knee.

Continue sweeping toward the bow, letting the rotational force of your unwinding torso swing the boat around.

Remove the paddle when it is almost to the gunwale. Think of the stroke as having moved the boat toward the paddle.

More Strokes

31

The first half of this stroke is identical to a reverse sweep. But midway through the stroke, you rotate the paddle and finish the stroke with the opposite side of the blade (the powerface), pushing against the water, as in a bow draw. This adjustment turns the boat without also pushing it backwards, as a reverse sweep often does.

Begin as you would a reverse sweep. Rotate your torso toward the stern, shifting your weight to your on-side knee, and place the paddle in the water behind you. Keep both hands low, control thumb facing out toward the water. Your shaft hand should be high on the paddle so you can place the blade farther from the boat.

Sweep the paddle forward in a wide arc, pushing against the water with the backface of the blade, with most of your weight still on your on-side knee. Follow the paddle with your eyes, so your head and torso rotate with the stroke.

As the paddle comes alongside your hips, instead of continuing with a reverse sweep, with the backface of the blade pushing against the water . . .

. . . flip the blade over in the water . . .

More Strokes

. . . by rotating the shaft so your control thumb is down . . .

. . . and, unwinding your torso, complete the stroke with the power-face of the blade pushing against the water, as in a bow draw.

A tandem sweep travels half the arc of a solo sweep because its purpose is to turn just one end of the boat. Extending a sweep through its full swing exerts turning force on the other end and counteracts what your partner is doing. The general rule, then, is that the arc of a tandem sweep stays between a point across from your knees and your end of the boat. Thus, a *bow forward sweep* begins exactly where a solo sweep does, but ends when the paddle is directly across from your knees, rather than continuing behind. Conversely, a *bow reverse sweep* begins alongside your knees, rather than as far back as you can reach, but ends where the solo version does. (Because this stroke slows the boat's forward momentum, it doesn't have as many applications as other tandem strokes, but it can be used in combination with a stern forward sweep to spin the boat to the on-side.)

The *stern forward sweep* begins across from your knees, rather than farther forward, and a *stern reverse sweep* ends alongside your knees, rather than continuing forward to the bow.

Tandem paddlers should use complementary forward and reverse sweeps to spin the boat on its pivot point. In fact, a combination of sweeps is the most efficient way to point a boat in a new direction.

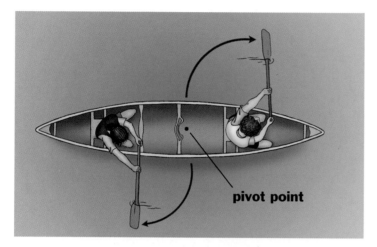

pivot point

The arc of a tandem sweep is about 90 degrees.

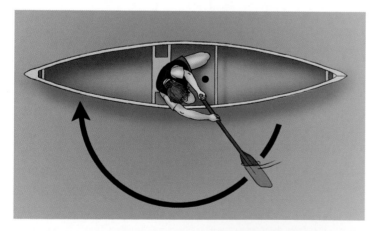

The arcs of both forward and reverse solo sweeps are about 180 degrees.

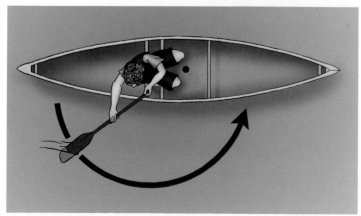

More Strokes

CROSS STROKES

Cross strokes are done on your off-side without switching the position of your grip and shaft hands on the paddle (unlike the sit 'n' switch technique, where your shaft and grip hands trade places as you pass the paddle over the boat). They are used by solo paddlers and the bow paddler—never the stern—in a tandem boat when an off-side stroke is needed immediately to change the direction of the boat, a situation that arises most often in fast water. The cross draw stroke, for example, is commonly used to pull the bow of the canoe into an eddy. The cross forward stroke can be used to stop an off-side turn, or alternated with forward strokes (instead of J-strokes or stern prys) to maintain a straight course when starting from a standstill.

Cross strokes use the powerface of the paddle, just like their on-side counterparts, and travel the same path through the water. However, they require more torso rotation and flexibility than normal strokes, because your shaft hand must reach all the way across your body. Another difference in form is that unlike conventional strokes, you should lean toward the paddle when doing a cross stroke.

If you paddle only in flatwater, you may never need a single cross stroke; if you paddle in fast water, you will use them all the time.

CROSS BOW DRAW   Pulls the boat toward the off-side

Rotate your torso to your off-side.

Plant the paddle across from your body, angled somewhat toward the bow, with the grip hand out over the water, control thumb pointed forward. Your grip hand should be at eye level and your shaft arm straight.

Cross Bow Draw (continued)

Now unwind your torso, bringing the boat toward the paddle.

Before the paddle gets to the hull, slice it forward and out of the water.

Rotate your torso to the off-side, bringing the paddle across the bow. Lean forward (an exception to the upright posture rule) and plant the paddle vertically, with your grip arm straight and your control thumb pointed inward across the boat.

Unwind your torso and straighten up . . .

. . . pulling your knees and hips past the paddle.

To recover, rotate the control thumb forward, turning the blade parallel to the hull. From there you can slice it forward through the water for another cross forward stroke or remove it for a return to your on-side.

More Strokes

37

BACK STROKES

Back strokes are used to move a boat backwards or simply to stop it from moving forward. There are a few variations, including the farback and the compound back, but since back strokes in general are little used and somewhat difficult to master, the basic stroke is all we show here. You can use it to move the boat back a few feet before peeling out of an eddy, to reposition the boat before going around a fast bend in the river, or just to maneuver a boat in tight quarters at a dock.

A word about when *not* to use the back stroke. Remember that a back stroke stops the forward momentum of the boat, and in a canoe, this means loss of control. If you use the back stroke to avoid an obstacle you're bearing down on in a river, you'll stall the boat and put the river in control. It's much better to use a stroke that steers the boat away from the obstacle while pushing you in the direction you want to go. That way, you maintain your forward momentum and use the current to take you where you want to go.

BACK STROKE Moves the boat backwards or stops its forward movement

Rotate your torso to the rear.

Plant the paddle behind your hips, backface forward, and your control thumb pointing out. Both hands should be over the water, arms bent.

Submerge the blade completely and push the paddle forward . . .

. . . keeping the blade vertical in the water.

Exit. If you're going to do another back stroke, rotate your control thumb to the rear at the end of the stroke, turning the blade parallel to the hull so you can slice it back to the catch position.

LOW BRACE

The low brace is a maneuver to keep a boat from capsizing when it has leaned too far toward your on-side. It involves a quick touch with the flat of the blade on the water, followed immediately by a weight shift the other way. It is important to understand that pressing the paddle against the water will not push the boat upright, but causes just a brief interruption in the boat's on-side roll. To reverse the roll, you must shift your weight. The key to the low brace is a matter of coordinating the timing of the paddle hit and the ensuing weight shift.

Most instructors teach the low brace with some reservation because beginners tend to overuse it in moving water, when they should be learning to rely on strokes and weight shifts. The problem is that to brace, you must stop paddling and you then give up the forward momentum necessary for directional control. In most cases, it's better to keep stroking and to control boat lean with your lower body. However, a quick brace can prevent a capsize, and as long as you don't use it as a replacement for good technique, it is a useful addition to your repertoire.

We show two versions of the low brace. The Canadian version is preferable in whitewater because it does not involve leaning as far out of the boat, and leaves you in a better position for a forward stroke.

LOW BRACE   **Prevents a capsize to the on-side**

As the boat leans toward your on-side, extend your paddle over the water, perpendicular to the gunwale. Both hands should be out over the water, knuckles down. Your grip hand should hit the water first.

As soon as your grip hand hits the water, begin pulling it up, pressing the backface of the paddle down against the water as flat as possible. Keep your head down over your grip hand.

Shift your weight to your off-side knee, and, if your boat has thigh straps, lift your on-side knee as you bring your grip hand back into the center of the boat. Keep your head down. This weight shift is largely responsible for righting the boat.

Back in business.

As the boat leans toward the water, rotate your shoulders toward your on-side and bring the paddle blade down against the water. Unlike the standard low brace, don't extend your grip hand out over the gunwale.

Lean forward and lower your head as you brace with the paddle, keeping your grip hand inside the boat.

Sweep the blade across the surface toward the bow, rotating your torso forward and shifting your weight to your off-side knee.

Don't bring your head up until your body is centered over the upright boat. Your paddle is now in position for a forward stroke.

More Strokes

Bow and stern paddlers in a tandem canoe use complementary strokes to turn the boat, and the basic repertoire of solo strokes covered in this chapter provide a myriad of combinations. The four combinations shown here are a good set to begin with: two turn the boat to the right, and two to the left. Practice them with a partner on flatwater to get the feel for how the boat responds.

The need for quick, powerful turns arises most often on rivers, where you have to steer the boat away from obstacles toward which the current is propelling it, get in and out of eddies, and make upstream maneuvers. In a fast current, you may get just one shot to make the right move, so a tandem pair with practiced complementary strokes is at a big advantage. The bow paddler may call for a turn or simply initiate one; the tandem paddler, seeing the stroke his partner has done, reacts with a complementary one.

Cross Bow Draw + Stern Pry. *Turns the boat sharply to the right. A good combination for punching across an eddy line.*

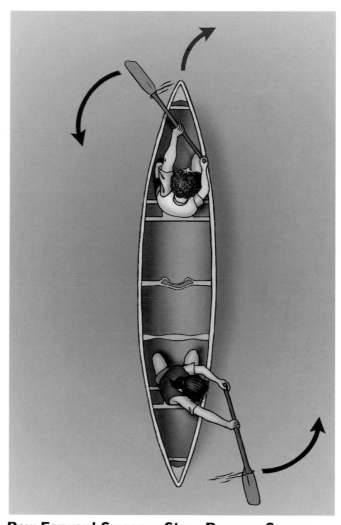

Bow Forward Sweep + Stern Reverse Sweep. *Spins the boat to the right (clockwise). Complementary sweeps are the fastest way for tandem paddlers to turn a boat around. Remember that a tandem sweep travels through half the arc of a solo sweep.*

More Strokes

Tandem Combinations (continued)

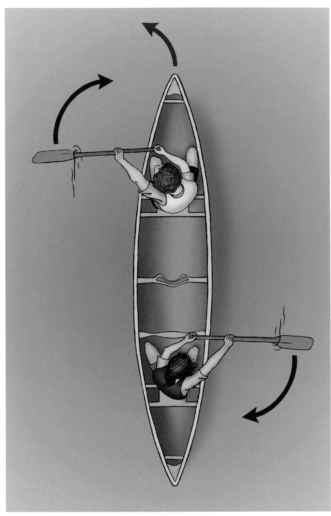

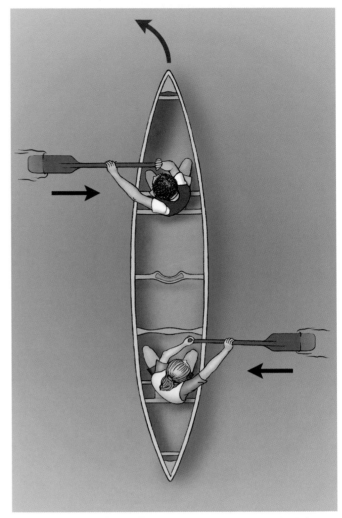

Bow Reverse Sweep + Stern Forward Sweep.
Spins the boat to the left (counterclockwise).

Stern Draw + Bow Draw. *Spins the boat to the left in a tight circle.*

4

On the Water

Paddlers divide water into two broad categories. Flatwater is the general term for water without current—a lake or a level stretch of river. Moving water includes everything from lazy rivers to frothing whitewater and is classified Class I through VI, according to the challenge it presents paddlers (see pages 60–61). Although kayaks and decked canoes have replaced open canoes as the boats of choice for whitewater, an open canoe is a natural river craft, and most people who own canoes wind up paddling on moving water at some point.

Whether you canoe on flatwater or moving water, you should understand the basics of water in motion.

Start with the fact that water is heavy and a large volume of it moving downhill or blown by the wind over long stretches has enormous power. This means, among other things, that even moderate changes in water level can significantly change the character of a river, and that wind is almost always a factor when canoeing on open water.

This book does not provide advanced whitewater instruction, nor does it cover wilderness touring or canoe camping. What we offer in this chapter are the basics of reading rivers and maneuvering easy to moderate rapids, as well as some guidelines for paddling safely on lakes.

The secret to paddling canoes on rivers is learning to work with the current, harnessing its power while avoiding its destructive force. And the first step toward that goal is understanding the basic properties of moving water and how it behaves when flowing around objects.

FACTORS AFFECTING CURRENT

Gradient, flow, and width are the three factors that affect the force of the current in a river.

Gradient is the slope of the river, expressed in the number of feet it drops per mile. A steeper riverbed creates a faster current. Precipitous drops are obviously dangerous, but what is less evident to beginners is that the force of the water increases disproportionately to the increase in gradient: if the gradient doubles, the force quadruples. Thus, even a slightly steeper stretch of river will be many times more powerful than a flatter stretch.

Flow is the volume of water carried past a point in a fixed amount of time, expressed in cubic feet per second

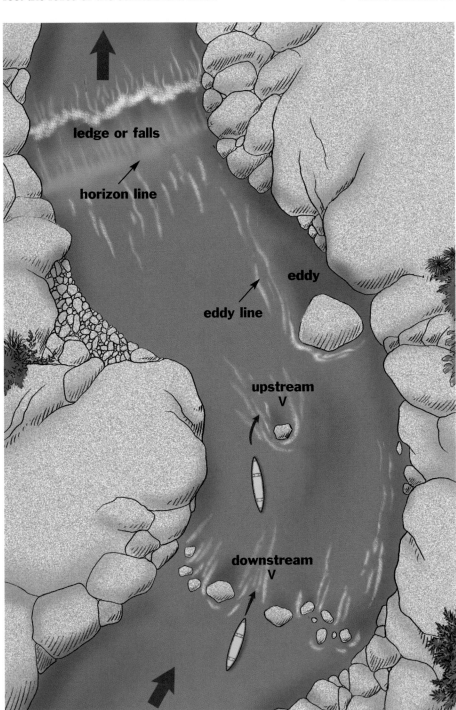

Look ahead as you approach any stretch of river and survey it for the best route. The water pointing downstream in smooth, V-shaped tongues is the path to follow: it points to channels between rocks. Conversely, upstream Vs point toward rocks. Learn to recognize this pattern from your vantage point in the boat, and plot a course following the downstream Vs. Remember to stay to the inside of bends. Also, note the position of eddies and the eddy lines that demark them. The eddy in this illustration would be the perfect place to pull over so you could get out and scout the falls below.

(cfs). Unlike gradient, flow is variable; it changes in response to rainfall and dam releases. But an increase in flow has a similar geometric effect on the force of the water: if the flow doubles, the carrying capacity of the water triples. A creek that's an easy float in June may have dangerous rapids in May. And at any time, torrential rain can quickly transform a placid river into a drowning machine. Before running a river, check river levels in local sources—newspapers, canoe club websites, outfitters, or boat shops.

Gradient and flow are related and must be considered together when evaluating the risk of a river. A river with a relatively low gradient—one that drops 10 feet per mile, say—may still be very powerful if it has a large flow. Conversely, some relatively low-volume streams have very steep gradients—several hundred feet per mile—that make them impossible to run.

Current is also affected by the width of the river. As the river narrows, the current speeds up, because the same volume of water is being squeezed through a tighter channel. A narrows or canyon may also have turbulent water where the currents from the wider stretch slam together.

CURRENT LANES

The current is faster in the middle of a straight stretch of river because there is less friction there than against the banks. The water in the middle also tends to be deeper, with fewer obstructions. So, as a general rule, you should paddle down the center of a river for a smooth ride, powered by the current.

However, when a river goes around a bend, most of the water is thrown to the outside, creating much faster current there and slower current on the inside. The fast current erodes the outsides of bends, undercutting banks and dredging deep channels, whereas the slow current drops sediment and debris on the inside of the bend, forming bars and shallower water. Another general rule, then, is to move to the inside of a bend. This involves looking ahead and taking action, because unless you do something, your canoe will be swept to the outside with the fast water. You'll have to watch for sandbars and shoals on the inside bank, but these are less of a problem than the turbulence and hazards on the outside, where the current can be treacherous. Also, because of the undercutting force of the water, the outside of a bend is more likely to hold submerged trees (see "Strainers," below) that have fallen into the water from the eroded riverbank.

ROCKS AND OTHER HAZARDS

Depending on their size, shape, and depth below the surface, rocks and other obstacles in the current pose a variety of problems to the paddler. How water flows around and over an obstacle—the froth, waves, or current lines it creates—will tell you how to approach it, and if you paddle on rivers, you should learn to recognize a few basic patterns.

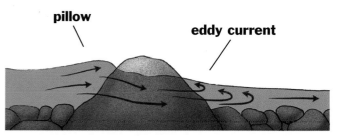

A large, rounded rock with its top above the surface has a buildup of water called a pillow *on its upstream side where the water hits it. The pillow is a benefit because it pushes a boat away. On the downstream side there may be a pocket of lower water and an eddy—an upstream flow circulating water back into the pocket.*

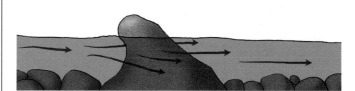

A rock with an undercut face has no pillow: the water flows around the rock beneath the surface. Any obstacle with an undercut face is extremely dangerous in fast water because it can suck a boat against it and trap it there. If you see a large rock in a swift current with no pillow above it, steer clear.

Downstream and Upstream Vs

The water pointing downstream in a smooth, V-shaped tongue is the path to follow: it points to a channel between rocks. Conversely, upstream Vs point to obstacles. Learn to recognize this pattern as you look downstream from your vantage point in the boat. Plot a course following the downstream Vs.

On the Water

Holes

A hole is the paddler's term for a depression below a submerged rock into which water is recirculating. Holes range from entertaining rides to hazardous traps, depending on the size and position of the rock and the volume of water pouring over it. A large volume of water pouring over a large, barely submerged rock or ledge with a sharp drop-off below it can create a deadly recirculating current called a hydraulic. Smaller holes are marked by standing waves just downstream of the depression and are relatively safe to run.

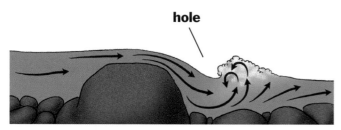

hole

A rock below the surface is marked by a hump of water with some degree of turbulence behind it, from froth to waves. If the water behind the rock is relatively shallow, a hole may form—a trough with a wave breaking back into it.

Lean into Rocks

A basic rule of river running is that *if you're being swept into a rock or obstacle in the water, lean into it.* Although your instinct may be to lean away, doing so lowers the upstream gunwale and presents the open boat to the onrushing current, which can fill the boat and pin it against the rock with such force that you won't be able to free it. But if you lean downstream, into the rock, the current will be pushing against the rounded bottom of the boat and won't have as much pinning force. Leaned this way, you'll be able slide off the rock, even if it takes some pushing with your arms or paddle, and continue downstream.

Hydraulics

A hydraulic is a strong recirculating force below a rock or ledge that can pull a boat or any buoyant object in and keep it there. One way to gauge the power of a hydraulic is to note the length of the eddy behind the rock or ledge. If the water behind a large submerged rock is moving back upstream from more than three feet away, it's too powerful to risk paddling through. Steer clear.

A large rock or ledge close to the surface with a lot of water pouring over creates a hydraulic—*a powerful recirculating force that can pull a boat in and keep it there.*

Particularly deadly hydraulics form below *low-head dams.* These dams may not appear dangerous; they're just low concrete walls with a smooth flow of water going over. But the volume of water is actually huge, and the force of the hydraulic this creates, as well as the fact that it stretches all the way across the river, creates an inescapable trough.

The Dock Street Dam on the Susquehanna River in Harrisburg, Pennsylvania, has claimed eleven lives since 1985. Most fatal low-head dam accidents occur when upstream boaters approach too close and are swept over, thrown out of the boat, and drowned by the powerful hydraulic.

Horizon Lines

A level, unbroken line of water across the river downstream of you may mean danger! It can signal a precipitous drop—a ledge, falls, or low-head dam—over which a large volume of water is flowing. Either the drop or the hydraulic behind a horizon line is a potential killer, and if you get too close, the strong current just above the ledge can pull you over. Learn to recognize horizon lines visually from upstream, and listen for the sound of a large volume of water going over a ledge. Paddle to shore and portage around or scout a safe route.

If you see an unbroken line across the water, as in this boat-level view taken upstream of Wesser Falls on the Nantahala River, pull over and scout the water ahead. A horizon line can signal a dangerous drop-off or low-head dam.

This is the view from the bank 100 feet downstream of the previous photo, showing Wesser Falls, Class IV water that only experienced paddlers in whitewater boats should attempt.

Strainers

A strainer is an underwater object, commonly a downed tree, that allows water to flow through it. Strainers are extremely dangerous because they "strain" the water while trapping objects, including people and boats, too large to pass through them.

Along wooded rivers, strainers are most often found on the outside of bends, where the fast water undercuts banks and uproot trees. Other submerged objects, including fences, cables, grates, or debris deposited by floods, can act as strainers and may be found anywhere in the river. Ask local paddlers about such hazards.

Rising water is another factor that can create strainers by covering brush and trees along the bank. Keep an eye on the river ahead, and stay away from strainers.

Downed trees are the most common form of strainer in a river. In swift current, they are dangerous because they trap objects—including people—too large to pass through the branches.

Waves

Unlike waves on lakes or seas, which travel across the water, waves in a river are stationary. They're created when fast moving water hits the slower moving water below it. This happens in a few different situations. A standing wave forms where a sheet of water plunging over a submerged rock or through a chute between rocks hits the slower water just below.

If the wave is tall enough to break back on itself, it's called a *stopper*, because it can literally stop a boat. Holes often have stoppers below them, but such holes aren't as dangerous as hydraulics because enough water is flowing through the hole to push your boat downstream after it's momentarily stopped by the wave. If the stopper is large enough, however, it can fill your boat with water.

A wave tall enough to break back on itself is called a stopper *because it can temporarily stop a boat. Commonly found below holes, stoppers are not particularly dangerous because enough water is flowing through the hole to send the boat downriver.*

A *wave train* is a regularly spaced series of waves that occur where deep, swift water is squeezed into a channel and piles up on the slower-moving water downstream. Wave trains are relatively safe to run because there are no rocks beneath them. In fact, they mark the channel and, hence, the best route to follow. The key to recognizing a wave train is the even spacing of the waves. Avoid a wave off by itself or out of alignment with the series: it marks a rock.

A wave-train is a regularly spaced series of waves that occur where deep, swift water is squeezed into a channel and piles up on the slower-moving water downstream. Wave trains mark the channel and—if the waves aren't too tall—the best route to follow.

In general, waves in a river are better approached head-on than at an angle, as in flatwater. Ride along the sides, or "shoulders," of the waves rather than their peaks. This head-on approach does make for a bouncier ride, but in whitewater the risk of broaching the wave (turning sideways to it) and swamping is too great.

Whitewater stretches can be a chaotic jumble of waves. Pull over and take the time to study such a stretch and plan a route.

EDDIES

An eddy is an area of upstream current created when the water in a river flows around an obstacle and then back to fill the depression behind the obstacle. Unlike a hole, the recirculating current in an eddy is on the surface. An *eddy line* marks the boundary between the upstream and downstream currents.

Recognizing eddies and getting in and out of them are the key skills in running rivers. In most cases, eddies are safe havens. Boaters use them as resting places and as way stations from which to scout the river below. As we have seen, the length of an eddy line can also signal the power of the hydraulic that created it—another important reason to learn to recognize an eddy current.

An eddy forms a teardrop shape behind an obstacle, the tip pointing downstream. An eddy's upstream current is strongest at the top, right behind the obstacle. The farther from the obstacle, the weaker the upstream current becomes, until eventually it dissipates altogether. Of particular significance to boaters is that the downstream current is strongest right next to the eddy line. Some instructors call this the "rejector line," because if you don't cross it with enough speed or the right angle, it will push your boat back into the main current.

For paddling in moving water, there are three general rules to keep in mind:

1. To maintain control you must move the boat faster than the current.

Once you lose your forward momentum, you go where the current takes you. So in doing river moves, it is not enough to float along and steer. You must point the boat where you want it to go and propel it there.

2. Lean the boat into turns.

The force of the oncoming current against the sides of a boat sitting flat in the water can flip it. Leaning reduces the chance of capsizing by lifting the opposite side of the hull and presenting the rounded bottom of the boat, rather than its straight sides, to the current. Lean the canoe by shifting your hips and knees; keep the upper half of your body upright. The combination of forward momentum and weight shifts will turn a boat much more effectively than even the strongest turning strokes in a slow-moving boat riding flat on the water.

3. Look ahead to where you want to go.

This is another application of the principle of vision discussed at the end of Chapter 1. If you're doing an eddy turn, look across the eddy line into the eddy itself and where you want the boat to arrive. If you're ferrying across the river, look to your destination on the far shore, rather than focusing on the square foot of water where you're planting your paddle or the rock right in front of you. This kind of vision will help you plan the best route and use the current to your advantage.

Cutting out of the main current into an eddy is the most basic skill in running rivers. It requires decisive paddling, good timing, and a basic understanding of eddy currents. The formula is: angle, speed, lean.

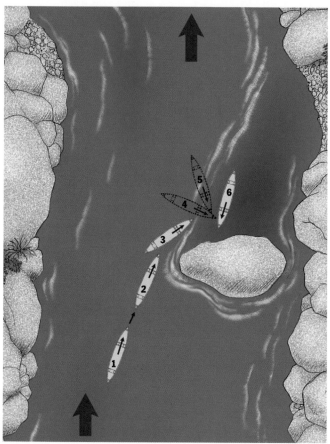

Overview of an Eddy Turn. *Enter the eddy at its upstream end, just beyond the rock or obstacle that creates it, and punch across the eddy line (3) at about a 45-degree angle.*

Angle

Hit the eddy line at a 45-degree angle, just downstream of the obstruction creating the eddy (which here we'll say is a rock). As you approach the rock and while still above it, position the boat far enough away from the rock to set an angle toward it, but not so far away that you'll be swept past the eddy. This entry point is important because you want to hit the eddy where its upstream current is strongest: right behind the rock. If your angle is too great—if you start perpendicular to the eddy line—the main current will sweep the stern downstream. If your angle is too little—if you're more parallel to the eddy line—you won't be able to punch through it. Setting the right angle is a matter of seeing ahead and of commanding the strokes you need to point the boat where you want it to go. Because the boat is moving forward throughout this maneuver, you'll have to set an angle that makes it appear you're headed straight for the rock. But by the time you get there, the current and your strokes will have moved you beyond it.

Speed

Paddle hard across the eddy line. You've chosen your entry point behind the rock because the upstream current is strongest there and will pull your bow into the eddy. But the downstream current is also strongest right along the eddy line, and it takes force to punch through it. Also, the water running off the upstream face of the rock creates a deflecting force. You must make short, powerful strokes to get the boat into the eddy.

Lean

Remember the mantra: lean into turns. This is important here because as you turn into the eddy, the main current is still pushing on the bottom of the boat and can flip it if you don't have enough angle, speed, and lean. Lean the way you would when going around a turn on a bicycle, and the downstream current will have less direct force against the sides of the boat.

Stroke Sequences for Eddy Turns

Use forward strokes to build up momentum for punching across an eddy line, and save the turning strokes for after you've crossed it.

A right-handed solo paddler entering an eddy on his right uses a stern pry just as the bow crosses the eddy line to keep the boat turned into the eddy. Once across the line, he plants a bow draw in the eddy to help turn the boat upstream, followed by a forward stroke to move the boat up into the eddy. The same paddler turning into an eddy on the opposite side would use a draw to turn the boat as the bow crosses the eddy line, followed by a cross bow draw to pull it into the eddy.

To turn into a right-side eddy in a tandem boat (bow paddler on left, stern on right) the bow paddler uses a cross bow draw and the stern paddler a stern pry to turn the boat as it crosses the eddy line. Then, the bow uses a forward stroke and the stern a reverse sweep to swing the boat up into the eddy. The stern may need to convert to a low brace at the end of the sweep to stabilize the boat. For a turn into an eddy on the other side, the bow paddler uses a draw and the stern paddler a forward sweep to begin the turn over the eddy line. The stern may then follow with a draw to complete the turn.

An important point about turning strokes in eddy turns: plant the stroke across the eddy line, in the eddy, not in the main current. Use your forward strokes to get you across the line.

Eddy turns take some practice. You'll miss a few. A common problem is waiting too long to start the turn and then finding yourself too far past the rock to catch the upstream current that pulls you into the eddy. But once you get the feel for them, eddy turns are fun and satisfying. They let you harness the power of the current.

Tandem Eddy Turn

1. The stern paddler initiated this eddy turn with a stern pry as the boat approached the eddy line from upstream with good speed. Here, as the boat crosses the eddy line, the bow paddler plants a cross bow draw inside the line. The correct angle of entry and sufficient forward speed allow this team to pull neatly across the eddy line.

2. The main current swings the stern around and boat crosses the eddy line.

3. The paddlers lean into the turn as the boat swings into the eddy.

4. Once the boat is in the eddy, the bow paddler switches to cross forward strokes and the stern paddler to forward strokes to push the boat upstream . . .

5. . . . into the slack water at the top of the eddy, where they can pause before moving on.

Solo Eddy Turn

1. With good angle and momentum, a solo paddler sets up to turn into the eddy behind the rock in front of him.

2. He leans into the turn . . .

3. . . . using a cross bow draw to steer the boat into the eddy . . .

4. . . . and a strong cross forward stroke . . .

5. . . . to pull the boat high into the eddy. The exaggerated forward lean used for this cross forward stroke would be bad form for an on-side stroke.

A peel-out is the maneuver for leaving an eddy and getting back into the main current. A peel-out is simpler than an eddy turn, in that you don't have to set up an angle at a moving target—the rock moving toward you. But peel-outs do require more powerful initial strokes than eddy turns, because you're starting from a standstill and can't use the main current's momentum the way you do approaching an eddy. The same angle-speed-lean formula applies.

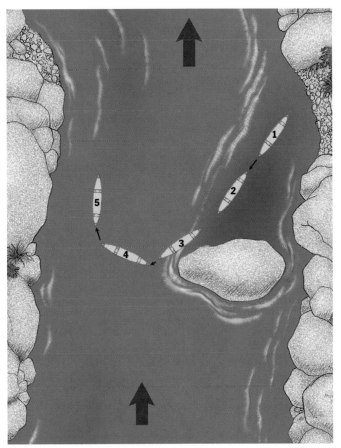

Overview of a Peel-Out. *Start well back in the eddy, parallel to the eddy line, and accelerate across the eddy line at its head, with the boat angled upstream. Lean into the turn and let the current swing the bow downstream.*

Angle
Your starting point is the key. Position the boat as far back in the eddy as you can without getting out of its upstream current, and stay no more than a foot or so inside the eddy line. Being far back gives you distance to build up momentum for breaking across the eddy line. Stay far enough inside the eddy to be able to exit at a 45-degree angle.

Speed
Dig into those initial forward strokes, remembering that power comes in the first burst after the plant. Breaking across the eddy line to exit takes forward momentum, just as it does for entering, but here you don't have the current pushing you.

Lean
As you break across the eddy line, shift your weight to your downstream knee and lean the boat into the turn. The main current will catch the bow, turning it downstream, and you can begin forward strokes. The most common cause of capsizing in peel-outs is the failure to lean into the turn. An upright boat will have its bottom pushed out from under it.

Stroke Sequences for Peel-Outs
The stroke sequence for leaving an eddy is similar to that for entering it: approach the eddy line with forward strokes, building up enough speed to cross it, and then use the appropriate turning strokes to point the boat downriver.

Bow paddlers and solo paddlers use bow draws or cross bow draws—depending on which side of the river the eddy is located—to turn the boat downstream once they've crossed the eddy line. A solo paddler—or stern paddler in a tandem boat—may also use a stern pry, stern draw, or forward sweep.

Just as in an eddy turn, it's important to plant this turning stroke on the other side of the eddy line—in this case, in the main current.

A beginner tendency in peel-outs is to use a brace to stabilize the boat as it leans downstream crossing the eddy line. But remember the first rule of moving water, about maintaining control. It's better to keep stroking forward, because when you brace, you aren't paddling and the current takes over.

Tandem Peel-Out

1. Starting far back in the eddy, both paddlers accelerate with forward strokes.

2. They power the boat toward the eddy line, building up as much speed as possible.

3. The boat crosses the eddy line at a 45-degree angle.

4. The bow paddler's cross bow draw helps swing the nose of the boat into the main current. Each paddler is weighting his downstream knee to lean the boat into the turn.

5. The bow paddler switches to a forward stroke as the boat turns downstream.

On the Water

54

Solo Peel-Out

1. Starting well back in the eddy, a solo paddler sets up for a peel-out.

2. With short, powerful forward strokes, he accelerates toward the top of the eddy.

3. He punches across the eddy line at a 45-degree angle . . .

4. . . . and switches to a cross forward stroke to maintain forward speed as the boat joins the main current.

5. Note the downstream lean of the boat, into the turn.

A ferry is a maneuver for crossing a river without moving downstream. It's an important skill, for you will often find yourself in situations where you need to go directly across the river. A common situation is when you're setting up to run a rapids and the safest line through starts from the other side of the river.

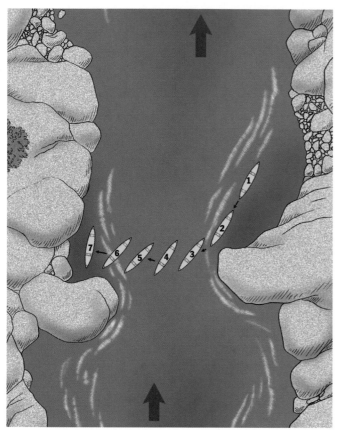

Overview of a Ferry. *Start well back in the eddy, as you would for a peel-out, but closer to the eddy line. Exit the eddy at the top, pointing almost directly upstream. Unlike a peel-out, don't let the current swing the bow downstream. Keep it pointed at an angle upstream as you cross the river.*

Angle

Setting and maintaining the right angle is crucial in ferries. If you set a course directly across the river, the current will take you far downstream of your target. If you set an angle course too directly upstream, you will fight the current the whole way. Aim for about 30 degrees or so, depending on the speed of the water: the faster the water, the more you must point upstream.

When you begin a ferry, you're usually sitting in an eddy, so the first move is to exit: start back in the eddy, parallel and next to the eddy line, and build up momentum with forward strokes. When you cross the eddy line, however, don't turn downstream as in a peel-out, but keep the boat headed upstream. If you hit the eddy line at too great a downstream angle, the main current will whip you around, ruining your angle for the ferry or even flipping the boat.

Once you're headed upstream in the main current, start paddling with forward strokes, letting the bow swing to 45 degrees across stream. It is much better to be pointed a little too far upstream ("too little angle") than too far downstream ("too much angle"), because it's easy to let the current swing the bow downstream but hard to push it back up against the current.

Lean

Lean the boat downstream by shifting your weight onto your downstream knee. When you get to the eddy on the far side of the river, shift your weight to your upstream knee as you cross the eddy line.

On-Side Solo Ferries

An on-side ferry is one in which your on-side strokes are on the downstream side of the boat—if your on-side is your right, for example, and you're ferrying across a river whose current is flowing from your left to right. Forward strokes in an on-side ferry have the advantage of turning you upstream a bit and helping you maintain the right angle. Additional upstream corrections are best made with stern draws.

Off-Side Solo Ferries

An off-side ferry is one in which your forward strokes are on the upstream side—if your on-side is your right, for example, and you're ferrying across a river with current flowing right to left. Off-side ferries are tougher than on-side, because you have to lean downstream while paddling on the upstream side. Also, your forward strokes tend to turn you downstream, making it harder for you to maintain an upstream angle. Use stern prys to swing the bow back upstream.

A general rule for solo ferries is to make short, powerful forward strokes followed by immediate, strong corrections—stern draws or prys—to hold the upstream angle.

Tandem Ferries

The added power of a second paddler is a great benefit in ferrying. The bow paddler does power strokes while the stern paddler maintains the angle with draws or prys, depending on which way the ferry is headed.

Back Ferries

A back ferry is used to reposition the boat, often to set the boat at a better angle for going around a bend. Back ferries are much easier in a tandem boat. The stern paddler sets the angle by prying or drawing the stern toward the opposite bank, and then both paddlers use backstrokes to take the boat upstream to the desired position.

Tandem Ferry

1. A ferry begins like a peel-out, with the boat in the eddy, facing upstream, parallel and close to the eddy line. These paddlers intend to cross the river to the eddy on the far shore, behind the large rock.

2. They accelerate with forward strokes and hit the eddy line pointing slightly more upstream than for a peel-out (compare the angle here to that in step 3, page 54). It's better to be angled a bit too far upstream than down at the beginning of a ferry because it's easy to let the current swing your bow downstream, but difficult to turn it back up.

3. The bow paddler uses forward strokes to power the boat across the river while the stern paddler maintains the upstream angle with stern draws. Notice that they're pointing the boat at a spot well upstream of the target   the eddy behind the rock—to compensate for the current pushing them downstream.

4. As the boat approaches the eddy, the stern paddler points the boat more perpendicular to the eddy line so the bow can punch across it. If the boat is angled too far upstream at this point, the strong current at the eddy line may reject it.

5. Once across the eddy line, the bow paddler uses a forward stroke to drive the boat up into the eddy.

6. Safely across the river, in the haven of the eddy.

Solo On-Side Ferry

1. An on-side ferry is one in which the paddler's on-side (in this case, his right) is facing downstream. The paddler begins the ferry well back in the eddy.

2. He powers to the head of the eddy using forward strokes . . .

3. . . . and breaks across the eddy line at an upstream angle.

4. Forward strokes in an on-side ferry help maintain the proper upstream angle across the river.

5. The paddler uses a stern draw to make downstream adjustments as he crosses the river and approaches the destination eddy.

6. A cross-forward stroke pulls the boat into the eddy.

Solo Off-Side Ferry

1. In an off-side ferry, where the paddler's on-side (in this case, his right) is facing upstream, it is more difficult to maintain speed and the correct upstream angle, because forward strokes tend to turn the boat downstream. Add this effect to that of the current, and you can quickly lose the correct upstream angle. This paddler leaves the eddy with a good upstream angle.

2. He maintains more of an upstream angle than normal as he starts across the river, using powerful forward strokes . . .

3. . . . followed by stern pries or rudders, the strokes most effective in off-side ferries across fast water.

4. Approaching the eddy, he maintains the upstream angle with a stern pry or rudder.

5. Just before entering the eddy, he points the bow almost perpendicular to the eddy line.

6. He uses a forward stroke to drive the boat into the eddy.

INTERNATIONAL SCALE OF RIVER DIFFICULTY

Developed by the American Whitewater Affiliation, this rating system is a general guide to sections of rivers. Specific ratings are necessarily subjective and inexact, because aside from depth and flow, river features cannot be quantified. Classifications also may vary according to region and the opinion of the evaluators. Furthermore, rivers change character according to rainfall, storms, and dam releases, so that a Class III rapids one day may be a Class V the next.

Use a rating as a guideline, but always check local conditions and get informed advice before attempting a new stretch.

Class I   Easy

Fast-moving water with riffles and small waves.
Few or no obstructions, all easy to avoid.
Risk to swimmers is slight.
Self-rescue is easy.

Class II   Novice

Straightforward rapids with wide, clear channels that are obvious without scouting.
Occasional maneuvering may be required, but rocks and medium-size waves are easily avoided by trained paddlers.
Swimmers are seldom injured, and group rescue, while helpful, is seldom needed.

Class III   Intermediate

Rapids with moderate, irregular waves that may be difficult to avoid and are capable of swamping an open canoe.
May include fast current and narrow passages that require complex maneuvers and good boat control.
Large waves, holes, and strainers may be present but are easily avoided.
Strong eddies and powerful current effects may be present, particularly on large-volume rivers.
Scouting is advisable for inexperienced parties.
Chance of injury while swimming is low, but group assistance may be needed to prevent long swims.

Class IV   Advanced

Intense, powerful rapids requiring precise boat handling in turbulent water.

Depending on the character of the river, there may be long, unavoidable waves and holes or constricted passages demanding fast maneuvers under pressure.

A fast, reliable eddy turn may be needed to navigate a drop, pull over and scout rapids, or rest.

Rapids may require "must" moves above dangerous hazards.

Scouting is necessary the first time the stretch is run.

Risk of injury to swimmers is moderate to high, and water conditions may make rescue difficult.

Group assistance is often essential but requires practiced skills.

The ability to perform a strong Eskimo roll is highly recommended. (This maneuver is beyond the scope of this book. Consult a whitewater paddling book or video.)

Class V   Expert

Extremely long, obstructed or violent rapids that expose the paddler to above-average risk of injury.

Drops may contain very large, unavoidable waves and holes, or steep congested chutes with complex, demanding routes.

Rapids often continue for long distances between pools or eddies, demanding a high level of fitness.

What eddies exist may be small, turbulent, or difficult to reach.

Several of the above factors may combine in the most difficult water of this class.

Scouting is mandatory.

Rescue extremely difficult, even for experts.

A very reliable Eskimo roll and above-average rescue skills are essential.

Class VI   Extreme

Features of Class V extended to the limits of navigability.

Nearly impossible and very dangerous.

Rescue may be impossible.

For teams of experts only, and only in favorable water levels after close study with all precautions.

The frequency with which a rapid is run should have no effect on this rating, as a number of Class VI rapids are regularly attempted.

On the Water

The most sensible and sometimes the only way to get around a river hazard is to pull ashore upstream of it, get out of the boat, and either portage around it or lead the boat through it on a line.

PORTAGING

Portages are common in longer canoe trips because of the greater chance of encountering unrunnable rapids or dams or the need to go overland between bodies of water. For a long wilderness trip, you will have studied the route enough to know the stretches that must be portaged. On any river, you should pull over and scout a difficult stretch to consider whether portaging around it is smarter than running it.

The two-person, right-side-up carry is fine for short distances, and especially over rough terrain, where an overhead carry would mean greater risk of dropping the boat. If you come to a hazard—a low-head dam or a short but dangerous rapid—pull to shore upstream, leave the gear in the canoe, and simply carry it downriver along the bank with one person at each end, as shown in Chapter 1.

For longer portages, unload the boat and divide the duties: one person carries the canoe in a solo overhead carry, while the other leads the way down the trail, packing the gear.

For solo overhead carries, most boats have a carrying yoke in the center that is shaped to fit the shoulders. You can use a PFD or towel on your shoulders for padding. If there is no yoke, or if you want more comfort for a long portage, lash paddles between the fore and aft thwarts (or between the bow thwart and portage yoke) about shoulder-width apart, and put padding on your shoulders. This setup allows you to adjust your balance point fore or aft and gives you a little more freedom in shifting weight over a long carry.

LINING

Lining is a strategy for getting around a hazard when you can't portage or don't really need to. One such situation is if you come upon a dangerous-looking rapid where the bank is too steep to pull the boat out for a portage. Another is a short rapid or hazard with relatively shallow water alongside it or a path along the river. In these cases, you can pull to shore, tie a line to the bow and stern, and, walking on shore or wading at the edge, lead the canoe through the bad stretch.

The person in front leads the canoe while the person behind keeps the stern from swinging broadside to the current. Always wear your PFD. Wading can be treacherous.

Wind and Waves in Open Water

Wind is the constant nemesis of boaters. It has increased effect over water, where there's nothing to stop it. Any boat gets pushed around by the wind, but a canoe is particularly susceptible because of its light weight, long hull, shallow draft, and flat bottom.

Two elements—fetch and wind speed—determine the force of the wind. Fetch is the distance the wind blows over open water. The greater the fetch, the greater the power of the wind and the bigger the waves. On a windy day, the end of a lake or bay exposed to a long fetch—the downwind end—will have much higher waves than the end from which the wind is blowing. This is more of a factor on big lakes than on rivers. However, a big river may have long, wide pools where the wind can be even more powerful than the current and actually blow you upstream.

Pay attention to wind direction when planning a trip. Keep in mind that early morning is the least windy time of day. Ask locals about prevailing winds on a big lake, and always check the forecast.

Whether traveling with or against a stiff wind, paddle at a quartering angle to the waves. This orientation lengthens the distance between crest and trough and smooths out the ride. If you hit waves head-on or paddle directly away from them, the boat will plunge up and down. If you travel parallel to the waves, the rocking action will bring water over the gunwales and may swamp the boat.

When navigating open water, plan a course along a shoreline sheltered from the wind, and stay close enough to land that you can get off the water if a storm blows in. Thunderstorms sweep across large expanses of water with alarming speed, and the middle of a lake is no place to be caught in an open canoe amid lightning and whitecaps. If you plan to cross open water, check the forecast beforehand, and once you're out there, keep your eyes and ears open for signs of approaching storms.

5

Boats, Paddles, and Gear

CANOES

No one canoe design is ideal for everything. A flatwater boat is not as maneuverable as a whitewater boat. A whitewater boat requires too much effort to keep it going straight to be a good flatwater boat. A fast cruiser can't carry enough gear for a camping trip. And so on. Many veteran paddlers own several boats for different purposes, but a specialized canoe is not the best choice for a first boat. You're better off with an all-purpose design that will perform acceptably on different types of water.

The four most common categories of canoe are recreational, touring, whitewater, and cruising. The best all-around beginner boats are from the first two categories.

Recreational canoes tend to be wide, stable, slow, and heavy, and are meant for beginners and casual paddlers on lakes and slow rivers. Touring canoes are designed for longer trips on lakes or rivers. They're lighter and not quite as initially stable as recreational canoes, but they're faster and stay on course better, while still holding a lot of gear. They make good all-around boats.

Whitewater canoes and cruisers are specialty boats. A whitewater hull is short and stubby, for maneuverability, while a cruiser is long and narrow, for straight-ahead speed. If you're buying a new canoe, the manufacturer will describe the purpose of each model.

If you're shopping for a used boat, however, a basic knowledge of hull features will help you assess a canoe's strengths and weaknesses.

Initial and Secondary Stability

A hull with initial stability is not tippy at rest or during casual paddling. Flat-bottomed boats with straight sides and hard chines have excellent initial stability. But such a hull design, if leaned far enough to one side, will reach a point of no return and flip; it has low secondary stability.

The reverse is true of a round-bottomed boat. It has less initial stability—it feels tippy because it's easier to rock from side to side—but in fact it can be leaned farther over than a flat-bottomed boat without flipping; it has good secondary stability. White-water boats, for this reason, have rounded bottoms.

Hull Features

Length and Width. A longer, narrower boat is faster than a shorter, wider one, and a longer boat "tracks" better: it maintains a straight course with fewer corrective strokes. However, a wider boat is more stable, and a shorter boat more maneuverable.

Canoes range in length from about 9 feet, for a solo whitewater model, to 18 feet, for a tandem flatwater cruiser. The "beam"—the width at the widest point of the hull—ranges from about 28 inches for a narrow cruiser to 37 inches for a wide recreational canoe. (Large transport canoes or models designed for hunters can be much longer or wider, but these are exceptions.) All-around canoes range between 15 and 17 feet long and 34 to 36 inches wide.

Rocker. The curvature along the bottom of a hull from bow to stern is called rocker (as in rocking chair.) A whitewater canoe has a lot of rocker, allowing it to turn easily because its bow and stern are out of the water and the boat pivots on a smaller area of hull. Flatwater boats, by contrast, have little or no rocker because a flatter bottom is better for keeping a boat going straight. An all-around boat often has mild rocker, a compromise that allows both turning ease and good tracking.

Shape of Bow and Stern. Blunt or "full" ends are better for whitewater because their greater volume, compared to tapered ends, lets them ride higher and keeps them from plowing under in turbulent water. Pointed or "thin" ends are better for flatwater cruising or racing because they slice through the water with less resistance.

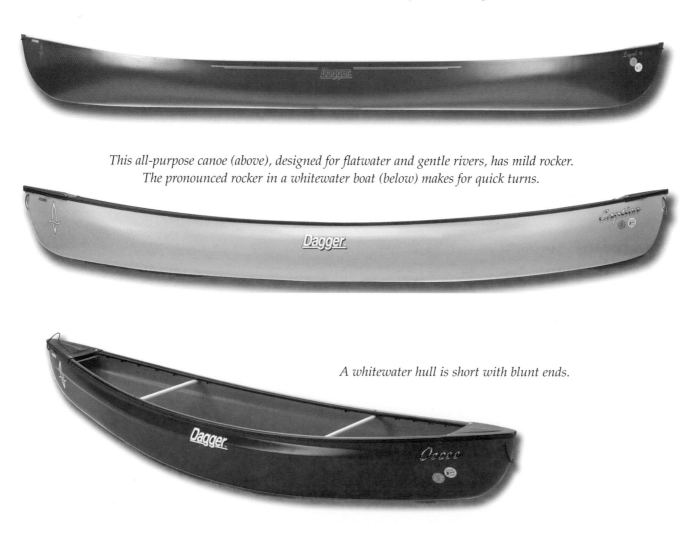

This all-purpose canoe (above), designed for flatwater and gentle rivers, has mild rocker. The pronounced rocker in a whitewater boat (below) makes for quick turns.

A whitewater hull is short with blunt ends.

Shape of Sides. A *flared* hull, in cross section, is wider at the top than at the bottom. The hulls of whitewater boats are flared because this design improves the boat's secondary stability and also keeps the inside drier by deflecting water that splashes against the hull.

Tumblehome refers to a hull that in cross section is narrower at the top and wider at the bottom—the reverse of a flared hull. Boats designed for flatwater cruising have this design because it allows the paddle to be held more vertically in the water, making for a more efficient forward stroke. Such a hull has less secondary stability, however.

Combination. The hulls of many canoes have flare at the ends, for stability and dryness, and tumblehome in the middle, for ease of paddling.

Straight. Many recreational and all-purpose canoes have straight sides.

Shape of Bottom. A flat-bottomed canoe has excellent initial stability but poor secondary stability. Such a design is acceptable for casual paddling on calm water. A flat bottom is desirable for activities like nature photography or bird watching, which require a stable platform.

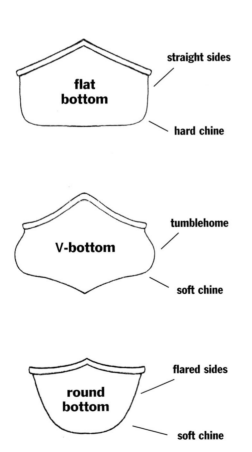

The elements of hull contour include the shapes of the sides, chine, and bottom.

A round-bottomed canoe is more maneuverable, easier to lean, and so is the choice for whitewater.

A V-bottom boat has low initial stability, but tracks very well—stays on course—and has excellent forward speed because it cuts through the water. The deeper the V, however, the harder the boat is to turn; a shallow-V hull makes a better all-purpose boat.

Most all-purpose canoes have a slightly rounded bottom—sometimes called a "shallow-arch"—that offers a good compromise between initial stability and maneuverability. Such a boat is at home on both flatwater and easy rivers.

Some boats intended for use on large lakes and almost all aluminum canoes (for manufacturing reasons) have keels—a ridge of material down the center of the hull that helps the boat stay straight. This feature, however, makes a canoe much less responsive to turning strokes, and thus hard to maneuver.

Chine. Chine is the shape of the hull, in cross section, at the transition from sides to bottom. A flat-bottomed boat with straight sides has a *hard chine*—almost a right angle—which contributes to initial stability. A round-bottomed boat with flared sides has a *soft chine*—a more gradual transition—and better secondary stability.

Canoe Materials

Note: Approximate weights listed below are based on a survey of general-purpose 16 1/2-foot canoes about 36 inches wide.

Royalex. A Uniroyal brand name, now generically used, for a laminate of ABS plastic, foam core, and vinyl coating. Royalex springs back to shape after being dented and also tends to slide off rocks. These qualities, along with its midrange price and excellent durability, make Royalex the most common material for whitewater and general-purpose canoes. A 16 1/2-foot Royalex canoe weighs about 65 pounds. Price range: $900-$1,500.

Polyethylene. A dense molded plastic, popularized as Ram-X in the Coleman line of canoes. Poly boats are indestructible, inexpensive, and heavy. A 16 1/2-foot model weighs 80 to 85 pounds. Price range: $400–$600.

Composites. Layered materials that may include high-tech synthetics like Kevlar, fiberglass, and carbon fiber. Composite boats are expensive and not quite as durable as Royalex. Their main advantage is weight. A 16 1/2-foot Kevlar composite canoe can weigh as little as 40 pounds. Price range: $1,400–$2,000.

Fiberglass. Weighs about the same as Royalex but is more brittle, a weakness that increases with age. Avoid used fiberglass boats. A 16 1/2-foot fiberglass canoe weighs about 70 pounds. Price range: $700–$900.

Aluminum. An aluminum canoe is fine for casual use in flatwater, but not for whitewater, where it can be permanently damaged in a crash. An aluminum hull does not slide off rocks like plastic and so is easily pinned against them in whitewater and tends to hang up in shallow rocky bottoms. Also, aluminum canoes have keels, which make them hard to turn. They're virtually maintenance-free. A $16^1/_2$-foot aluminum canoe weighs 70 to 75 pounds. Price range: $600–$900.

Wood. Wooden canoes are beautiful, expensive, relatively fragile, and maintenance-intensive. They are not suited for whitewater. If the aesthetics of wood and traditional design appeal to you, you can find several companies still making fine wooden canoes. A $16^1/_2$-foot wooden canoe weighs about 70 pounds. Price range: $1,200–$3,500.

Recommendation: To learn basic strokes on flatwater, almost any canoe will do. Borrow or rent whatever you can find. But when you go to buy one, consider the kind of water you'll be paddling on, study the market, and buy the best boat you can afford. A heavy old clunker or a specialty boat in the wrong kind of water can ruin your experience in a hurry. And as with other types of equipment, a brand name tends to hold its resale value.

For your first canoe, shop for a used Royalex boat by an established company such as Dagger, Mad River, or Mohawk, between 15 and 17 feet long and about 36 inches wide. It should have two seats, and the hull should have slight rocker and flared sides. If you'll be paddling solo on rivers, get a boat on the shorter end of the range with a bit more rocker, for better maneuverability. If you'll be traversing lakes or paddling tandem most of the time, go for a longer boat with less rocker.

PADDLES

Material. Paddles with aluminum or fiberglass shafts and plastic or fiberglass blades are maintenance-free, indestructible, and inexpensive. A good choice for the beginner. You can get a good one for around $20.

Wooden paddles are preferred by many for their feel and look. High-quality wooden paddle blades are laminated from several types of wood to achieve strength and light weight. Wooden paddles for whitewater use have shafts wrapped with fiberglass, for abrasion resistance, and blade edges reinforced with synthetic materials. Price range: $80–$300.

Paddles of Kevlar, graphite, and other synthetics combine light weight with strength and are expensive.

Whitewater paddles tend to be thicker and heavier than flatwater paddles, because they take more abuse.

Grip. A T-grip is a good choice for the beginner and for whitewater paddling because it allows a firmer grip and more precise blade control.

(1) *Bent-shaft paddles are designed for efficient, long-distance flatwater paddling.* **(2)** *A sturdy, inexpensive model with aluminum shaft, plastic blade, and T-grip. The broad, square-ended blade is the most common shape for all-around use on rivers and lakes.* **(3)** *Laminated wooden blade with plastic rock-guard on the tip.* **(4)** *Beavertail blade with pear grip. This is a traditional design for flatwater, but not appropriate for fast water, because the blade doesn't catch as much water and the grip doesn't allow as much control.*

Sizing the Paddle

A rule of thumb for correct paddle length is that standing next to the paddle with the tip on the ground, the grip should come up to your chin. A better way to measure is to sit in the canoe and immerse the blade to its throat. The grip should then be at about nose or eye level. For most people, the right shaft length is somewhere between 54 and 59 inches.

All of the above are general rules. In practice, the correct paddle length varies with the body proportions and style of the paddler, and the best way to find the right length for you is to try different paddles on the water. Definitely do this before buying an expensive model.

Traditional flatwater paddles have pear grips, which allow the grip hand more freedom of movement.

Blade. The blade of a whitewater paddle is relatively short and wide and is squared off at the end. It's designed for quick, powerful turning strokes where the paddler must grab a lot of water.

A flatwater blade is longer, narrower, and more rounded at the tip, designed for continuous forward strokes and feathering at the end of the stroke. The paddle is lighter than a whitewater model.

Bent-Shaft Paddles. Designed for long-distance flatwater paddling and marathon racing, bent-shaft paddles increase the efficiency of the forward stroke by allowing the blade to enter the water farther forward and to stay at a power angle farther through the stroke. They're also easier to remove from the water at the end of the stroke because the blade is more vertical than a straight-shaft paddle at this point. The paddle is used only with the blade angled forward. Only one side of the blade is usable as the powerface. Bent-shaft paddles are not good for turning strokes or for any stroke that uses the backface of the paddle for power, such as a stern pry.

PFDs

A Type III (vest-type) PFD is required by law for boaters in most states and by the American Canoe Association for participation in its courses. It's smart to wear a PFD any time you get into a canoe and it's an absolute necessity for whitewater paddling.

A PFD designed specifically for paddling, rather than for water skiing or general boating, has armholes large enough to allow freedom of movement. The vest must be adjustable so that it won't slip up over your head. It should have at least 15.5 pounds of flotation. Individual buoyancy varies according to a person's physiology and the water conditions, but most adults need

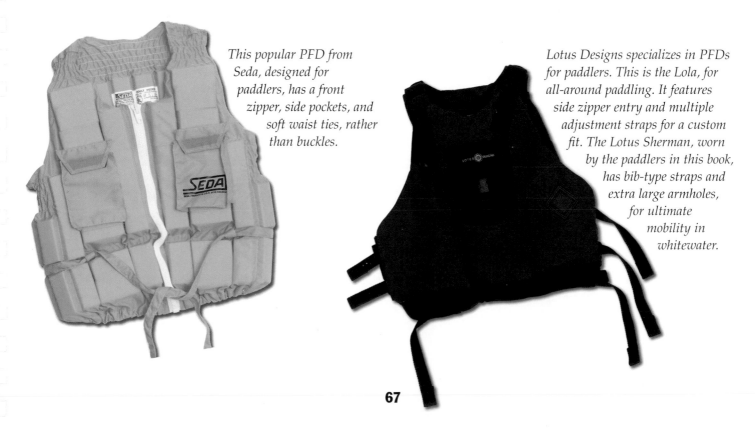

This popular PFD from Seda, designed for paddlers, has a front zipper, side pockets, and soft waist ties, rather than buckles.

Lotus Designs specializes in PFDs for paddlers. This is the Lola, for all-around paddling. It features side zipper entry and multiple adjustment straps for a custom fit. The Lotus Sherman, worn by the paddlers in this book, has bib-type straps and extra large armholes, for ultimate mobility in whitewater.

only about 10 pounds of additional flotation to keep their heads above water.

Good PFDs start at about $40. Cheaper ones may meet basic safety requirements but will not fit as well and may chafe at the arms. Paddling a long way in an ill-fitting or poorly designed PFD is torture.

Try on a PFD before your buy it. Sit down, adjust the side straps for a snug fit, and have someone pull up on the vest at the shoulders. If it slides above your head, try another model or one with a crotch strap. You should also simulate paddling movements by rotating your arms in wide circles, then crossing them over your chest. If the vest chafes or bunches up anywhere, try another size or model.

Don't use your PFD as a cushion. Compression of the flotation material reduces its buoyancy.

RIVER GEAR

Spare Paddle. Always keep a spare paddle fastened to the inside of your boat.

Helmet. A paddling helmet has an outer shell of plastic, a foam lining, and a chin strap. It can prevent serious injury if you're thrown from the boat and your head hits a rock, the boat, or any other hard object. Your head is especially vulnerable if the boat rolls in rapids. You absolutely must wear a helmet if you're wearing thigh straps in a whitewater boat that's likely to roll, intentionally or not. Always wear a helmet in fast, rocky water or anything above Class III rapids.

A helmet is a necessity in Class III water and up, or wherever spills and flips in rocky water are likely. This model is from Shred Ready.

Knee Pads. The recommended kneeling position can be hard on the knees after even a short while. There are two remedies: strap-on kneepads, like those used by gardeners or athletes, or foam pads glued to the bottom of the boat. If you'll be doing a lot of paddling in the kneeling position, it makes sense to affix pads to your boat. Foam kneepads are widely available as accessories from canoe manufacturers and outdoor sports retailers, and they're inexpensive. If you make your own, use closed-cell, nonabsorbent foam with a nonslip surface.

Thigh Straps. Thigh straps are a standard feature on whitewater boats and can be added to any boat to give the paddler better control in leans, turns, and braces. They let you "wear the boat," making it much more responsive to body movements, such as when you dip your on-side knee into a turn while lifting your off-side knee, or when you lift your on-side knee to right the boat after a low brace. They also make strokes more efficient by preventing your body from slipping around and thus letting you transfer all the energy to the stroke.

Thigh straps are attached to the bottom of the boat and are placed over your thighs with fast-release clips. They should not trap you in the boat; you must be able to extract yourself in a capsize.

Saddles and Toe Blocks. A variety of other accessories are available to customize your position in the boat, including toe blocks, which give your feet something to push against, and kneeling saddles of molded foam.

Flotation. A canoe will float when filled with water, but without added flotation, it will sink to its gunwales, making recovery difficult, especially in fast water. A canoe filled with water is much heavier, harder to tow, and more prone to being pinned against obstructions than one that rides higher. Also, if swamped, a boat with some of its interior packed with flotation takes on less water and therefore remains somewhat maneuverable.

Inflatable nylon flotation bags can be bought for the ends as well as the center of the boat. The minimum flotation for whitewater solo boats is two 30-inch end bags, one each under bow and stern deck. End bags are triangular, shaped to fit under the deck, and should not extend far enough into the boat to interfere with the paddler's feet. A tandem boat needs an additional bag in the center.

Float bags must be securely tied in place or they'll pop out. Lash-down kits are available from bag manufacturers, or can be homemade. The system includes eyelets or holes in the gunwales, through which cord is crisscrossed, and tie-down loops glued to the floor of the boat, which hold down the ends of nylon straps that buckle over the bags.

A fully equipped whitewater boat is very responsive to a paddler's movements and weight shifts. The molded foam saddle and toe blocks hold him securely in the cockpit, and the thigh straps allow him to lift one side of the boat as he weights the opposite side, a great advantage when leaning into turns. The flotation bags fore and aft displace water when the boat is flipped or swamped, letting it ride higher and lighter.

End Lines. End lines ("painters") are lengths of rope attached to the bow and stern. They're used for tying boats to docks or vehicles, leading canoes through rapids, and holding onto during self-rescue in fast water (see page 75). A painter should be 15 feet of $1/2$-inch polypropylene, because this material floats. Choose a bright color, for visibility. Longer lines—up to 25 feet—are useful for lining boats through rapids. Tie lines securely to the bow or stern and store the excess in the bottom of the boat, held down with an elastic cord or tucked under an air bag. Storage of painters is important in whitewater. If they're just thrown loosely into the bottom of the boat, they can get tangled up in gear and be hard to pull out during self-rescue. Or, they can wind up trailing behind the boat while you're paddling, where they can entangle a swimmer or catch on a tree limb.

Throw Bag. A nylon bag containing rope that can be thrown to a swimmer. The bag serves several purposes. It's a compact storage container for the rope, a projectile easier thrown than a loose rope, and it contains flotation, making it easier for a swimmer to grab. The bag should contain 60 or 70 feet of brightly colored $3/8$-inch polypropylene rope. Throw bags are available commercially or can be homemade.

Whistle. A whistle can be heard above the roar of a rapids or by members of a party around a bend in the river. Clip one to your PFD for whitewater trips.

Knife. A knife in a sheath clipped to your vest can be a lifesaver if you or someone in your party goes overboard and becomes tangled in a tow rope or painter. If you choose a folding model, make sure you can open it with one hand, if necessary. Stainless steel is best for blades that will be used around water.

Dry Bags and Boxes. Various size waterproof bags and boxes are available from camping and paddling supply retailers. If you do a fair amount of canoe camping or river running, it makes sense to buy some for the equipment that must stay dry, including electronic gear, cameras and binoculars, and spare clothes.

Plastic trash bags work fine to store clothes and other nonfragile gear. Buy a thick gauge, and double-bag items that must stay completely dry. Don't pack the bag too full: leave at least a 1-foot neck free to tie an overhand knot.

Bailer and Sponge. One way or another, water finds its way into the floor of a canoe. It drips from the paddle, it's blown in as spray, it comes over the side when you hit a wave. Or it rains. A bleach bottle with the bottom cut off makes a fine bailer, and is especially useful after a flip, when there's a large volume of water to remove. A big sponge is handy for wiping up smaller amounts, and can double as padding or a packing wedge.

A throw bag from Salamander with 70 feet of $3/8$-inch rope.

First Aid Kit. First aid kits should be stored in waterproof containers, and kits for boaters are available in dry bags.

Carabiners. These quick-release clips, sold in the hardware departments of many stores as well as in climbing and outdoor shops, are handy for clipping dry bags, float bags, and other gear to the thwarts of a canoe or to your PFD.

CLOTHING

In warm weather on easy water, cutoff jeans and old sneakers are fine. But the dramatic effect of water on body temperature makes clothing choices important in any situation that involves the possibility of a dunking along with even moderately cool air temperature. The wrong clothes can, at best, make you miserable, and at worst, threaten your life.

Paddling clothes must allow you to swim. Avoid thick, bulky, or tight-fitting clothes. Layers of lighter, looser-fitting garments are better.

The only garments that will keep you warm while you're actually in the water are wetsuits and drysuits. Wetsuits are one-piece neoprene outfits (like scuba divers wear) that trap a thin layer of body-heated water between suit and skin. They're clammy and uncomfortable out of the water. Drysuits are made of waterproof fabric with elastic seals at neck, wrists, and ankles. They're more comfortable and, worn over a layer of pile fiber, will keep you warm in the water.

If you plan to run challenging rivers regularly, you may want to invest in a wetsuit or drysuit. But in most situations, you should choose clothes that will keep you warm in the boat, allow you enough limb movement to swim, and will dry quickly after you're out of the water.

Inner Layer. The first warning about outdoor clothing is that cotton kills. It absorbs water and takes forever to dry. If you fall overboard or get caught in a rainstorm in a T-shirt and jeans, you'll have wet fabric clinging to your skin the rest of the day. On a hot day, this may feel good at first. But if the river runs through a shady stretch or if you're still on the water when the sun dips below the trees, you will be cold, and if the air temperature is low enough, perhaps dangerously so. On

any paddling trip, assume you'll get wet, add that effect to the air temperature, and dress accordingly.

Wool or a synthetic fiber like polyester is best as an inner layer because these fabrics don't absorb water and they dry quickly. Long underwear of polypropylene is a good choice for longer day trips or overnighters in cool weather.

Middle Layer. Fleece or wool sweater.

Outer Shell. Jacket and pants of waterproof material are musts for trips of any distance. They block wind and rain and, worn over a wool or synthetic inner layer, keep you warmer than a thick single layer. Breathable waterproof fabrics are worth the money for the comfort and level of waterproofing they provide.

Footgear. Old sneakers are fine for canoeing. You may never need anything else. But a wide range of paddling footgear is available, and the right pair can make your trip more comfortable. Paddling shoes or booties are more flexible than sneakers, provide better traction against the bottom of a boat or the river, and drain more quickly. Water sandals are comfortable in warm weather because water flows through them. Neoprene booties will keep your feet warm in cold weather.

Hat, Sunglasses, Sunscreen. The effects of the sun when you're out on the water are multiplied because of surface glare and the lack of shade. The most harmful sunlight occurs between 11 A.M. and 3 P.M. Severe sunburn significantly increases the chance of skin cancer. Always wear a billed hat. (In cool weather, bring along a wool or polyester ski hat.) Polarized sunglasses reduce glare on the water and help you see obstructions below the surface. Use waterproof sunscreen of SP30 or higher on your face and any other exposed skin.

Gloves and Pogies. A number of manufacturers offer gloves designed for paddling. In addition to keeping your hands warm and dry, they'll protect against blisters if your hands aren't paddle-toughened. "Pogies," fingerless hand coverings that attach to the paddle, are also available from paddling gear suppliers.

Spare Clothes. On a trip of any length, or in cool weather, pack a dry bag with spare clothes, including sweater or fleece, socks, and hat.

6

Safety and Rescue

The enormous power of moving water and the debilitating effect of cold water on body functions are two factors that, alone or combined, can turn a boating mishap into a life-threatening situation. Inexperience and poor judgment add to the danger.

For thorough references on river rescue and wilderness first aid, consult the Resources section (page 87–88). We present here the basic safety and rescue guidelines that should be required knowledge for every paddler.

So, you've had some paddling training and experience, you're properly dressed, you're wearing your PFD, you're sober, and you can swim. Are you safe to run a stretch of water with Class III rapids? You're a lot safer than someone failing any of these basic tests, but there are other risk factors to consider, many under your control. The most important single rule of paddling safety is to use good judgment. Don't venture into unknown waters that may require more skills than you possess, and don't go alone.

5 Factors Associated with Boating Fatalities

Statistics show five factors recur in boating fatalities.

1. Lack of PFD
At the scene of fatal boating accidents, PFDs are often found inside a swamped boat or floating beside it. Failure to have a PFD, or to wear it, is a common ingredient in drownings.

2. Cold Water or Air
Hypothermia caused by immersion in cold water is a leading cause of death in boating accidents. Such accidents often occur in the spring, when the air temperature is warm but the water is still cold, and boaters are not dressed warmly enough. Layered clothing of the right fabrics is essential in cold weather, especially when water is involved.

3. Inexperience
Inexperienced paddlers with no formal training are more likely to be victims of fatal accidents than trained, experienced paddlers.

4. Alcohol
Alcohol is a leading contributor to boating fatalities, as it inhibits both coordination and judgment.

5. Inability to Swim
Nonswimmers are more frequent drowning victims than swimmers.

Adapted from *The American Canoe Association's Canoe and Kayaking Instruction Manual* by Laurie Gullion. Used with permission of Menasha Ridge Press.

THE RIVER PADDLING GROUP
Three boats is the minimum recommended number for running a river with even moderate rapids. The lead boat should have strong paddlers with experience at reading water, and ideally someone who knows the river and can show the way. The trailing or "sweep" boat should have strong paddlers with training in rescue and first aid, in case anyone in a preceding boat goes overboard. The weaker or least experienced paddlers should be in the middle boat or boats. The middle boats should never pass the lead boat or fall behind the sweep boat.

Boats should stay in sight of each other but not so close as to inhibit another boat's maneuvering. Fifty to 150 feet is the recommended distance between boats in whitewater. Communication is key. The middle boats must relay information from the lead boat to the sweep boat. Whoever spots a capsized or missing boat must relay that information to the rest of the party immediately.

Before the trip, assess each member's skills and condition against the demands of the route—in particular, the hardest stretch—and don't include someone with marginal or unknown skills. A rapids several miles from the put-in spot is not the place to discover that a member of the party lacks the paddling skills or physical condition to negotiate the route. He or she could jeopardize others by causing a spill and forcing a rescue in dangerous water.

SCOUTING THE ROUTE
Before You Go. The best way to orient yourself to the water is to bring someone who has paddled the route or to talk to someone who has. Otherwise, consult guidebooks, maps, local canoe clubs, or paddling shops for river information.

In using guidebooks, remember that river ratings are general guidelines that should be supported with specific information. You cannot assess the nature of a stretch solely on its difficulty rating. Fifty feet of Class III water is much less challenging than a full mile of it. Also, if a stretch is run mainly by kayakers, it tends to be rated slightly lower, because kayaks are built for whitewater. Again, talk to someone who knows the river.

Check the river level on the day of the run. Levels vary dramatically with rainfall, drought, or dam releases, and there is no way to know the state of a river

Emergency! Help!

Paddle, PFD, or helmet waved overhead. Three long blasts on a
    whistle.
Means: "Assist the signaler as quickly as possible."

Stop!

Arms held straight out to sides, flapped up and down, or paddle
    held horizontal overhead and pumped up and down.
Means: "Potential hazard ahead."
Pass on signal to other boats in the party and wait for all clear
    signal before proceeding.

All Clear

Paddle, turned flat, or arm, raised in vertical bar above the head.
Means: "Come ahead." In the absence of other directions, proceed
    down the center of the river.
To signal paddlers which side of the river to run to avoid rapids or
    an obstruction, tilt the vertical "all clear" toward the side of the
    river with the preferred route. Never point toward the obstacle
    to be avoided.

Attention

A series of short chirps on the whistle.
Used when no emergency exists but where the need to
    communicate is obvious and necessary.
This signal should not be given casually—only when other
    forms of communication are not working.

Safety and Rescue

on a particular day without checking. A river that's a pleasant float in mid-June may be a dangerous torrent in early May or a backbreaking haul over rocky shoals in August.

Also check a map to see where roads are in relation to the river, in case you have to pull out and go for help in an emergency.

On The River. Once you're headed down the river, always stop to scout the following situations:

- **Long or difficult rapids.** Pull to shore or into an eddy at the top of the stretch and survey the big picture, looking first to the end of the run, to see where you'll exit. Then work visually back upstream, connecting the route. Once you begin the run, take the boat from eddy to eddy—a technique called "eddy-hopping"—scouting below at each stop. If a stretch contains a hazard where boats are likely to spill, a few paddlers should walk downstream and position themselves where they can throw ropes to swimmers.

- **A blind corner.** If you can't see around the bend, pull over, get out, and walk downstream to a vantage point.

- **A horizon line across the river.** A horizon line signals a hydraulic or low-head dam. If scouting shows no safe route through the hazard, portage around it.

Flips in moving water are often sudden and followed by a confusion of overturned boats, swimmers, and floating equipment. Though it's natural to go after the expensive canoe floating toward a falls or the dry bag holding your good camera, every paddler should have the following rescue priorities fixed in mind: *people, boats, equipment.*

Rescue the swimmer first. If he's in a nonthreatening situation, go for the boat. Often they can be rescued together. But be prepared to abandon the boat if it's putting you in a dangerous position or if all your attention must be focused on the swimmer. Lastly, retrieve equipment.

On a calm lake or slow river when the water is warm, there may be time to gather things in whatever order is convenient. But in any situation, focus on people first.

SAFE SWIMMING POSITION

If you go overboard in fast water, roll onto your back and float with your legs downstream, feet out of the water. This position lets you fend off rocks with your feet, and is much safer than floating or swimming head first. Never stand up in fast water that is knee-deep or deeper. Your feet can be entrapped in rocks, and the current can knock you over and hold you under. This is a common cause of drowning among inexperienced whitewater paddlers who capsize. Situations in which you should abandon the safe swimming position:

- If you see a route to shore through safe water, roll to your stomach and swim for it.
- If you're being swept into a strainer—a downed tree or other obstruction with water flowing through it—turn around, approach it headfirst, and pull yourself up onto it with your arms. If you don't, the force of the current may drive you into the strainer below the surface and entrap you. Remember that strainers are dangerous because the water flows through and not around them.
- If the water is shallow enough, you may be able to stand up and walk to shore, but don't risk foot entrapment in fast water above your knees.

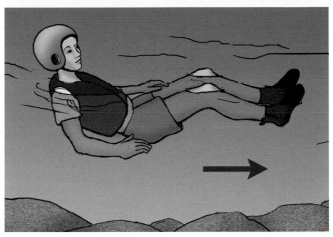

In most situations, lying on your back, facing downstream with your feet out of the water is the safest position in which to float through rapids.

STAYING WITH THE BOAT

If your boat is within reach after you go overboard, stay with it if you can do so without endangering yourself.

The first rule of swimming with boats in moving water is stay upstream of the boat. After a flip, a boat is usually filled with water and very heavy, and if you're downstream of it, it can pin you against an obstruction. A water-laden canoe pushed by a strong current has the force of a bulldozer. Don't get between it and a rock.

To stay with the boat, approach from downstream and grab the stern or downstream painter or grab loop. Never wrap the rope around your wrist; you must be able to release it immediately. If you float through rapids holding onto the painter, stay behind the boat at a safe distance. And be ready to let go of the boat if it's dragging you into a dangerous situation. You can replace the boat.

If there's a clear path to an eddy or the shore, swim to it using sidestrokes or backstrokes, towing the boat. If you can right the boat before towing, do so. A righted boat, even one swamped with water, moves more easily through the water than one that's upside down.

ROPE RESCUE

Rope throwing is an essential rescue technique for paddlers who run rivers. Every canoe in a party should carry a throw bag and every paddler should be practiced in throwing one. Putting a throw bag where you want it takes a little practice. Before a whitewater trip, each member of the party should spend some time tossing a throw bag at a target. You may get only one shot in a critical situation.

Two general rules of rope rescue: (1) Never tie a rope to yourself, whether you're the thrower or swimmer. You must be able to release the rope if it's pulling you under. (2) Carry a knife. Cutting a rope may save a life in the case of entanglement.

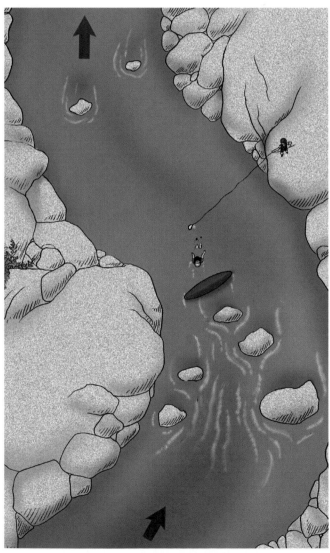

The rope thrower is positioned downstream of a likely capsize spot. He throws the rope when the swimmer is still upstream of him, aiming the bag over the swimmer or just downstream of her. It is better to throw long than short.

Position of Thrower. Rope-throwers may already be stationed along a difficult rapids, waiting for boats to come down. If not, a boat may have to go ashore to perform a rope rescue. In either case, the rope-thrower should choose a position on shore downstream of the swimmer, in a clear spot with solid footing, and ideally one in which the swimmer can be pulled into calm water or an eddy.

The Throw. First yell to the swimmer to get his attention. Then pull a few feet of rope from the throw bag and hold it in your nonthrowing hand. When you're ready to throw, yell "Rope!" and fling the bag toward the swimmer with an underhand toss. The rope should land a little downstream of the swimmer, so he's floating toward, not away, from it. Throw long, not short. The swimmer can grab the rope if it goes over him, but a short throw may land out of his reach.

Use an underhand toss, holding the tag end of the rope with your nonthrowing hand.

Hauling In. Once the swimmer grabs the rope, pull him in hand-over-hand, walking downstream and away from the river if you can. If you need more support to resist the pull of the swimmer, you can place the rope around your waist, a technique called a "body belay." Keep the tag end of the rope on the upstream side of your body and the end that goes to the swimmer on the downstream side. Otherwise, the rope can tighten around your torso as the swimmer is carried downstream. Wearing a PFD and gloves will protect you against rope burns when belaying. But use a body belay only as a last resort. It's better to remain mobile.

Swimmer's Grip and Position. The swimmer in a rope rescue should hold the rope to his chest—never tie or wrap it around any part of his body—and roll over on his back with the rope over his shoulder while being pulled in. If he faces forward on his stomach, his face will get the full force of the water, and if he ducks in this position, his head will be towed under.

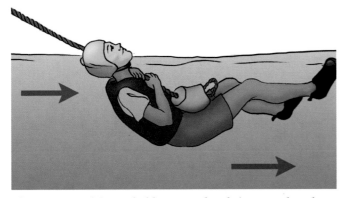

The correct position to hold a rope when being towed to shore.

A head-first position will pull your head under water.

REACH-THROW-ROW-TOW-GO

When a paddler goes overboard and you're faced with a rescue decision, remember this lifesaver's adage. The preference proceeds from shore-based, to boat-based, to water-based rescue.

REACH. First try to reach the swimmer while standing on shore.

THROW. If you can't reach him, throw him a rope.

ROW AND TOW. If you have no rope or he's too far away to reach with a rope, paddle or row out to him and tow him in.

GO. The last resort is going into the water after a swimmer, which is the most dangerous option, especially for someone untrained in lifesaving.

Towed Rescue. Towing a swimmer to shore from a canoe is very difficult in fast water because of the great drag the swimmer creates. The weight of the towed swimmer also pulls the stern of the boat upstream, making it hard for the paddlers to maintain a ferry angle to shore. Finally, an open canoe's vulnerability to swamping make it a poor craft for towing.

However, if the water is slow enough and there is enough distance before the next downstream hazard, a towed rescue is possible from an open canoe. The paddler(s) should throw the stern painter to the swimmer and paddle hard for shore. The swimmer can help by kicking his feet.

A word of caution: a panicked swimmer may try to board a canoe by grabbing the gunwale and can swamp the rescue boat in the process. It may be best to keep the boat out of grabbing distance of a swimmer in this state. Throw him the painter and coach him along.

If you flip a canoe on flat-water and there are boats close by, hang on to your canoe till they reach you. If the water is cold, get as much of your body out of the water as possible by crawling onto the hull. Water conducts heat away for your body much faster than air, even if it's windy. To conserve body heat, curl up in the HELP position (Heat Escape Lessening Posture): knees tucked against chest with arms crossed over them. If there are two or more people in your group, huddle together, facing each other.

If you are stranded in cold water away from the boat, the HELP position will conserve body heat. It only works if you're wearing a PFD.

If there are no boats around, swim for shore if it's close enough, but consider this decision carefully. The shore of a large lake may be farther away than it looks, and hypothermia dangerously impedes swimming ability.

If the shore is too far away, try to get back into the canoe. If the canoe has overturned, reach over the middle of the hull, grab the far gunwale, and pull it toward you until the boat flips right-side up. You'll then have a righted canoe full of water. You can crawl back in the swamped canoe and begin bailing, or use the following method to empty water from it before reentering. First, push down on either the bow or the stern of the canoe, submerging that end and lifting the other out of the water. Then shove the canoe forward forcefully. Some water will slosh out. Swim to the side of the boat and perform a similar move: push down on the near gunwale with both hands, sinking that side, and then push forward, hard.

SOLO SELF-RESCUE, DEEP WATER

Reentering a canoe is an awkward maneuver without someone to hold down the opposite side. It's especially tricky if the canoe is empty, with no water inside to stabilize it. Keep in mind, however, that it's also difficult to empty a canoe from the inside without a bailing scoop. Whether the boat is full or empty, use the procedure shown in the illustrations to crawl across the gunwales and swing your legs and backside in.

Once back in a swamped canoe, bail enough water

to make paddling manageable. If you don't have a bailer, and the boat is full of water, you can flip some out with your paddle or by rocking the boat carefully from side to side.

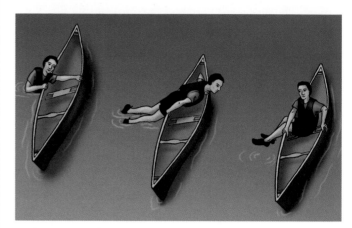

Position yourself at the center of the boat. Holding the near gunwale with one hand, reach across and grab the far gunwale with the other hand.

Use scissors kicks to boost your hips over the near gunwale, and then pull yourself across the boat.

Roll over into a seated position.

BOAT-OVER-BOAT RESCUE

Two canoes can work together to empty and right a swamped boat with this move, sometimes called the gunwale-over-gunwale rescue. It can be done by two solo canoeists, though more people are helpful to steady and roll the boat. The swamped boat must first be turned upside down, if it's not already.

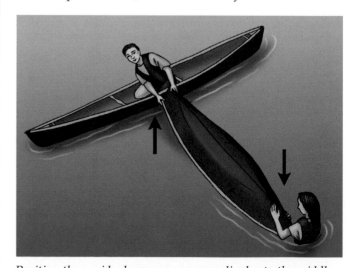

Position the upside-down canoe perpendicular to the middle of the rescue boat. The swimmer pushes down on the stern of the swamped canoe while the person in the boat lifts the bow over the gunwale. This move breaks the water seal and positions the swamped boat for recovery.

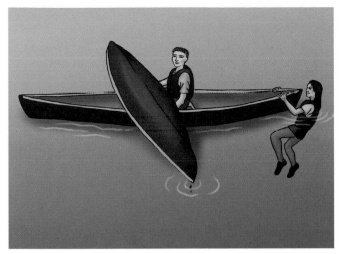

With the swimmer stabilizing the canoe from the rear, the seated paddler pulls the overturned canoe hand-over-hand across both gunwales of his boat.

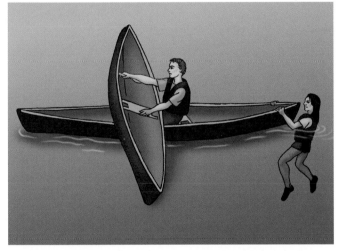

The seated paddler rolls the canoe away from him onto its bottom.

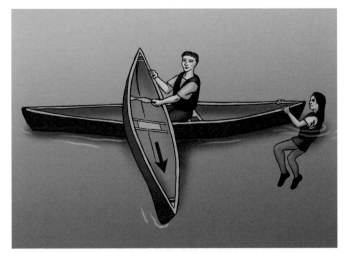

He then slides the boat back into the water.

The seated paddler holds the gunwale of the empty boat, tilting the boat toward the swimmer to make it easier for her to get her body across the gunwale on her side.

When her weight is over the boat, he pushes down on the near gunwale, scooping her into the boat as she rolls into a seated position.

Anyone going on an extended paddling trip, especially through remote areas, should take a first aid course offered by the American Red Cross. A number of excellent first aid books are available for reference (see the Resources section).

Training in cardiopulmonary resuscitation (CPR) is strongly recommended for anyone who paddles frequently. Victims of near-drowning have been resuscitated even after extended periods (in one case, more than an hour) underwater.

The purpose of this section of the book is to familiarize you with the main medical problems associated with paddling.

Hypothermia

Hypothermia is the cooling of body temperature to 95 degrees Fahrenheit or lower by exposure to cold air or water. Moderate hypothermia can be debilitating, and a severe case can cause death. Since water conducts heat away from the body thirty-two times faster than air, immersion hypothermia is of particular concern to boaters. It can occur even when the air temperature is warm. A summer dunking in a cold stream or lake, coupled with wind, rain, or cool evening temperatures, can bring it on.

Uncontrolled shivering is the first sign that a person is becoming hypothermic. As his body temperature continues to drop, his speech may become slurred, his motor skills and coordination may be impaired, and his behavior become irrational. Suspect hypothermia if a person who has been cold for a while begins stumbling or acting strangely. In the final stages of hypothermia, when the body temperature drops below 90 degrees, shivering stops, and the victim is in grave danger.

The treatment for hypothermia is common sense: warm the victim. If his condition is from exposure to the air, add layers of clothes, get him out of the wind, and give him food and water. In severe cases, place him in a sleeping bag until help arrives.

A victim of immersion hypothermia—that brought on by immersion in cold water—should be removed from the water immediately and changed into dry clothes. Immersion hypothermia is a common contributing factor in drowning because it comes on fast and makes swimming and paddling difficult or impossible.

Shoulder Dislocation

A shoulder dislocation is a painful and temporarily debilitating injury that occurs when the ball of the upper arm is knocked out of its socket. Paddlers are particularly vulnerable to this injury because their arms operate in a wide range of motion and are connected to a paddle that can be wrenched around by the force of water or jammed against a rock. Dislocations are more likely to occur when the arms rotate behind the body, or are held overhead or away from the body. Prevention, therefore, is largely a matter of good paddling technique: using body rotation rather than arm reaching to perform strokes, and keeping the arms within the paddler's box (see pages 8–9). Paddlers should also avoid reaching out or behind to fend off a rock with the paddle. With the upper arm away from the body, the force of the paddle hitting the rock can knock the arm out of its socket.

A dislocated shoulder can be slipped back into place on site by someone trained in the technique. Consult a wilderness first aid book. Otherwise, the arm should be placed in a sling and the victim taken to a doctor.

Tendinitis

Tendinitis, another common paddling ailment, is an inflammation of the lining around the tendon that can be quite painful. It most commonly afflicts the forearms and the rotator cuff of the shoulder. Paddlers who take a long trip after a period of inactivity are most vulnerable. Stretching, exercise, and pretrip training will reduce the chance of tendinitis. Treatment involves rest and anti-inflammatory drugs such as ibuprofen.

Cartopping

Canoeing inevitably involves putting a boat on a vehicle. Although a makeshift rack consisting of foam blocks between the canoe's gunwales and the car roof will work for an occasional short trip, if you do any amount of traveling, you'll want a roof rack. Such a rack will protect the roof of your car and provide secure tie-down points.

Tie down the canoe with four ropes or straps: two across the boat and one at each end. Tie-down kits with straps and buckles make the process quick and easy, but be aware that metal buckles can scratch your car or slap you in the face when you toss them over the roof. The system shown here uses ³/₈-inch rope and a few simple knots.

• Put the canoe on the roof of the car

Shown here is a solo side-mounting technique that is quick and easy but requires a certain amount of strength. The alternative is to load the canoe on the roof from the rear of the car. To do this, set the canoe upside down on the ground behind the car, lift the bow, and set it on the rear bar of the roof rack. Then walk to the stern, lift it, and push the boat forward onto the rack.

1. Approach the car from the side.

3. Step out from under the boat, tilt it away from you so it slides on the gunwale, and . . .

2. Raise the canoe off your shoulders and set one gunwale on the roof rack.

4. . . . push it onto the rack.

• Tie the canoe to the car with two lines over the hull

First, tie two lines to the side bar of the roof rack. (When cutting these ropes to length, consider if you'll ever be hauling two canoes. If so, cut the lines long enough to reach over both.)

1. Tie one end of each rope to the roof rack with a figure-eight knot.

2. Toss the ropes over the canoe, to the other side of the car.

Figure-Eight Knot

1.
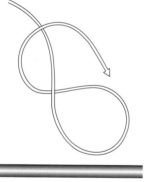

2.
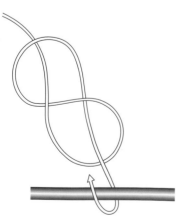

3.
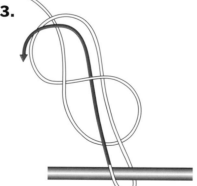

4.
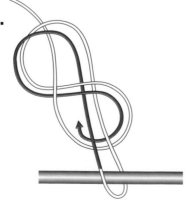

5.
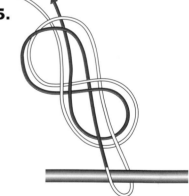

6.
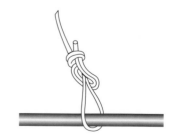

On the other side of the car, tie a traveler's hitch in each rope, lead the tag end through it, and tie each rope to the end of a cross bar with half hitches.

1. Twist a loop in the rope.

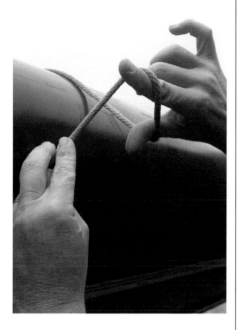

2.

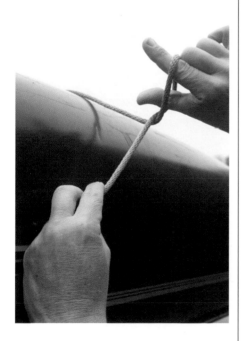

3. Reach through the loop, and pull a second loop through the first, cinching it tight.

4.

5. Position this loop at the bend in the hull.

6. Bring the tag end of the rope under the roof rack post . . .

7. . . . through the loop . . .

8. . . . and pull it down as tight as you can.

9. Secure the rope to the post with two half hitches.

Half Hitch

1.

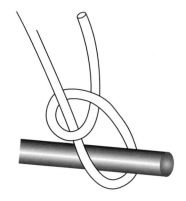

2.

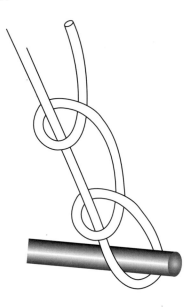

3.

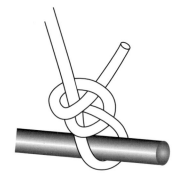

• Tie the bow and stern of the canoe to the front and rear bumpers of the car

If your canoe already has painters attached, you can tie these to the bumpers. If not, tie ropes to the grab loops at bow and stern of the canoe with figure-eight knots and then to the tow rings underneath the bumper. If your car lacks tow rings, tie the ropes to slots in the bumper or frame.

When you're finished tying down the canoe, it should be tight to the top of the car. If it moves when you push on it, tighten the ropes.

Resources

BOOKS

A select list of titles that cover topics beyond the scope of this book.

The Canoe Handbook. Slim Ray.
    1992. Stackpole Books.
    A standard reference from a former Nantahala instructor. Particularly valuable as a whitewater primer. Excellent explanation of river features and maneuvers.

Canoeing and Kayaking Instruction Manual. Laurie Gullion.
    1987. ACA/Menasha Ridge Press.
    The American Canoe Association's official guide. Strokes, maneuvers, safety and rescue, instruction guidelines. Black-and-white line drawings and diagrams.

NOLS Wilderness First Aid, 3rd ed. Tod Schimelpfenig and Linda Lindsey.
    2000. Stackpole Books.
    A standard in its field, developed by the National Outdoor Leadership School. Comprehensive guide to diagnosing, treating, and transporting patients in the wild, including information pertinent to paddlers, such as treatment for hypothermia, near-drowning, shoulder injuries.

Paddle Your Own Canoe. Gary and Joannie McGuffin.
    1999. Boston Mills Press.
    A beautiful book by a Canadian paddling team. Both a celebration of canoeing and a comprehensive guide to strokes and maneuvers. Superb, step-by-step color photos.

Path of the Paddle: An Illustrated Guide to the Art of Canoeing. Bill Mason.
    1995. North Word Press.
    A classic by a legendary Canadian wilderness canoeist. Comprehensive, detailed instruction on strokes and maneuvers, with extensive black-and-white photo sequences.

River Rescue: A Manual for Whitewater Safety, 3rd ed. Les Bechdel and Slim Ray.
    1989. Appalachian Mountain Club.
    The definitive guide to river rescue methods and gear.

MAGAZINES

Canoe & Kayak
10526 NE 68th Street, Suite 3
Kirkland, WA 98033
www.canoekayak.com

Paddler
PO Box 775450
Steamboat Springs, CO 80477
www.paddlermagazine.com

ORGANIZATIONS

American Canoe Association
7432 Alban Station Blvd., Suite B232
Springfield, VA 22150
703-451-0141

American Whitewater
    (formerly American Whitewater Affiliation)
1424 Fenwick Lane
Silver Spring, MD 20910
866-262-8429
www.americanwhitewater.org

United States Canoe Association
www.uscanoe.org

SCHOOLS

Most paddling schools devote much or all of their instruction to kayaking. The following programs from across the country offer courses in canoeing.

Boulder Outdoor Center
2707 Spruce St.
Boulder, CO 80302
800-364-9376

Kayak & Canoe Institute
University of Minnesota, Duluth Outdoor Program
10 University Drive
Duluth, MN 55812
www.d.umn.edu/umdoutdoors

Nantahala Outdoor Center
13077 Highway 19 West
Bryson City, NC 28713
800-232-7238

Wild Waters Outdoor Center
1123 Route 28
Warrensburg, NY 12885
800-867-2335

Zoar Outdoors Paddling School
Mohawk Trail, PO Box 245
Charlemont, MA 01339
800-532-7483

OUTFITTERS AND TOUR ORGANIZERS

Hundreds of canoe liveries and outfitters are listed on the website of the Professional Paddlesports Association, a nonprofit trade association.

www.propaddle.com

MANUFACTURERS

The companies below carry full lines of canoes or paddles in a range of styles and prices. For a more extensive list, check the annual buyer's guide issues of *Paddler* and *Canoe & Kayak* magazines, published at the beginning of the year.

Carlisle Paddles
PO Box 488
4562 North Down River Road
Grayling, MI 49738
989-348-9886
www.carlislepaddles.com

Dagger Canoes and Kayaks
Watermark
111 Kayaker Way
Easley, SC 29642
800-627-1568
www.dagger.com

Harmony Gear
Watermark
111 Kayaker Way
Easley, SC 29642
800-627-1568
www.harmonygear.com

Mad River Canoes
Confluence
3761 Old Glenola Road
Trinity, NC 27370
800-390-0819
www.madrivercanoe.com

Mohawk Canoes
963 CR 427 N
Longwood, FL 32750
407-834-3233
www.mohawkcanoes.com

Old Town Canoes
58 Middle Street
Old Town, ME 04468
www.otccanoe.com